Writers and Heroines

Essays on Women in French Literature

edited by
Shirley Jones Day

PETER LANG
Bern · Berlin · Frankfurt a.M. · New York · Paris · Wien

Die Deutsche Bibliothek – CIP-Einheitsaufnahme

Writers and heroines :
essays on women in French literature / ed. by Shirley Jones Day. –
Bern ; Berlin ; Frankfurt a.M. ; New York ; Paris ; Wien : Lang, 1999
ISBN 3-906761-61-4

Cover design by Philipp Kirchner, Peter Lang AG

ISBN 3-906761-61-4
US-ISBN 0-8204-4214-3

© Peter Lang AG, European Academic Publishers, Berne 1999

Printed in Germany

Writers and Heroines

Foreword

This volume of essays has its origins in a conference held at the Institute of Romance Studies of the University of London in March 1996. Its theme, an ambitious one, was the image of woman in literature from the Middle Ages to the twentieth century. Its aim was to open doors of discussion, not only on to periods of literature where the woman writer remains a shadowy figure, but also between different periods of literature and different critical approaches to the question of women as writers and heroines.

I would like to express my gratitude to my colleagues, Professor Annette Lavers and Professor Michael Worton, for their advice and encouragement during the planning of the conference. My sincere thanks are due to the French Embassy, whose Cultural Attaché, Monsieur René Lacombe gave the generous financial assistance that helped to make the conference possible. I would also like to thank Raymond Howard for his invaluable advice during its planning stage. That these essays now see the light of day in published form is due almost entirely to the computing skills and inexhaustible patience of Michael Bridgeman: to him we all owe a great debt of gratitude.

Three of the essays, those of Rosalind Brown-Grant, Jonathan Mallinson and Shirley Jones Day, are due to appear, either in their entirety or in abridged form, in the *Journal of the Institute of Romance Studies*, vol. 5 in June 1998. We are grateful to the editorial board for allowing us to print part or the whole of material due to be published in their journal.

Shirley Jones Day
UNIVERSITY COLLEGE LONDON
March 1998

Table of contents

Introduction:
From footnote to mainstream

The highest praise which can today be given to any piece of literary history or criticism, after two decades which saw numerous additions to their traditional objects as well as the reappraisal of value-systems which had generated such unaccountable gaps, is that they have helped to change the canon. This is a book which eminently deserves such praise. As Shirley Jones Day and her colleagues show, some works dealing with feminine destiny, although successful in their day and essential to understand important cultural transitions, have been interpreted in conventional ways or even been excluded from the literary pantheon and reduced to footnotes. The following chapters, written by male and female critics and devoted to the analysis and appraisal of various female authors and heroines often rescued from oblivion, all play their part in the current movement which, while seeking to redress an injustice or to learn from telling inconsistencies in the plots of novels, lives and reputations, in fact also contributes to clarifying and affirming some essential contemporary values.

They do so in a style which has itself been recognized as innovating in the last twenty years since it combines a freedom from established critical stereotypes with a careful parsing of nuances, gaps and discrepancies in novelistic discourse which point to 'unthought' or 'unsaid' ideals which our present experience alone can identify and describe. This is because we are dealing here with a history of oppression, whose study, like that of many other submerged areas of human experience which have recently been reclaimed by cultural history, necessarily generates a new methodology in order to make visible the tacit coercion often ruling at once the story, the characters' fates and the social and rhetorical conventions which programme the reader's understanding.

That this oppression bears on men as well as women goes without saying, and these studies are not lacking in examples of male authors and characters left to struggle with uncertain identities, hopeless dilemmas between passion and social acceptability or the very legibility of their desires within the context of available social roles. The intellectual panoply which has in recent years been added to literary history — psychoanalysis, a modernised rhetoric and poetics, an awareness of folklore and mythology — stands the critic in good stead when it comes to supplying the missing link in many jarring discourses and restituting a coherence which makes the stories of both sexes intelligible in both their historical and their eternal dimensions. Yet it is perhaps supremely in the realm of discourse that the fates of both genders may be most conspicuously different. Women all too often appear bereft of voice, whether this applies to authors who have simply been expunged from the literary canon or to characters who are denied by the reigning paradigm of woman the right and possibility to express a lucid awareness of their predicament, let alone of remedies they might conceive. Yet trying to perceive and interpret this missing voice may lead us today to unexpected conclusions which have topical as well as scholarly relevance.

'An idea called "woman" may be seen as the Leading Lady in the Story of Story, the development of the novel': this statement of Nancy Miller's finds definite support in the following studies, largely devoted to aspects of 17th- and 18th-century fiction. But it is a story with unexpected twists. The direct filiation between 17th-century women writers who are now, like their books, largely forgotten (except for *La Princesse de Clèves*, a model whose justified fame generated for this very reason, as we see here, some deceptive intertextual effects) and major 18th-century male novelists such as Prévost and Rousseau (not to speak of Richardson) takes place in a context which does make the earlier novelists look like 'orphaned heroines' such as Mme d'Aulnoy's character Julie.

The fate of female characters is no less characterised by silences and ambiguities, even if novelists of either gender reveal a common awareness of both social expectations and their drawbacks. For if female novelists mostly speak the alienating code of moral conservatism so that subversive aspects have to be unearthed by the attentive critic, male novelists who endorse that same code and outline stylised 'euphoric' and 'dysphoric' trajectories of female destinies, often cannot help implicitly favouring their condemned heroines by a sympathetic portrayal, or the admired rendering of passionate speech which will make many readers assume that the *religieuse portugaise* is a real woman since such 'bad', incoherent writing makes art conventionally unrecognisable. And as one of the authors remarks here, many male writers paid for the freedom to write their personal *sylphide* with her life.

But even a 'euphoric' destiny as it was then conceived does not for us compensate for the silencing, even the discouraging of women's awareness of their true position, which is a litany of losses. This has important artistic consequences. Let us for instance take the not infrequent case where a heroine, deprived of such advantages as birth, social class, legitimacy, wealth, and other attributes which would allow her to marry in a way satisfying her emotional and social aspirations and the innate nobility which she feels in herself. Since an explicit awareness of her self-worth would contradict the imperative of modesty and disinterested virtue which can alone excuse her disruptive beauty, she is forced into a displaying strategy which, while being the only way to play the very poor hand she has been dealt, robs her of her sincerity, since she has to simulate the lack of an awareness which is in fact directing her behaviour. Despite the common approval of self-possession and 'prudence', the latter would otherwise be construed as machination and be therefore self-defeating. This insoluble conundrum governing not only social survival but sometimes survival itself, devalues authenticity and makes problematic an identity unlikely to come here as it does in Joyce through 'silence, exile and cunning'. Against such a solid social code, any individual *parole* is bound to appear destructive and aberrant, not truthful or creative. It is therefore difficult to endow this type of heroine with any kind of authentic speech, and a third-person discourse has to be pressed into service. The lack of ontological equality which pervades even the socially happy ending in this underlying Cinderella grid can only be resolved on the plane of fantasy through a fairy godmother, who alone can repair the havoc caused by a myth in the first place.

A realistic text, where Cinderella and her Prince cannot simply 'marry and have many children' can use, however, another solution. The heroine can, and often is, a (rich) widow. Célimene, Araminte, Merteuil, Madame de Chartres, and several others described here, are thus empowered to fulfil their destiny up to a point, in ways which have not always been perceived because matrimony, prescribed by the 'fairy-tale' code, is still for many modern readers the ultimate ideal it represented for their suitors. When Mme de Beaumont writes a sequel to an unfinished novel by Mme de Tencin and gives it an ending which superficially resembles that of *La Princesse de Clèves*, we may thus miss its true meaning. A reading which does not see this ending as a sacrifice may instead show the heroine as desirous to secure for herself, as we would say, some 'space' in order to keep control of her own life, to refuse in fact to be a wife in order to be, quite simply, a woman (an *équivoque* favoured by the French *'femme'*). No wonder if this valorisation of female celibacy, chosen not from a fear of life, but from a lust for it in the limited sense allowed by the period, has to be rather obliquely expressed, remaining perhaps invisible to its very author. The same applies in a general sense to the paradigmatic status of the widow. This figure, indispensable for authors wishing to portray a free and complete woman but nonetheless essentially deprived (even Merteuil, intrepid as ever, chooses to stress the visibility of this freedom rather than its various furtive aspects) is an embarrassing metonym for a state of affairs which has endured well beyond the period studied here and which did not admit of fully satisfactory outcomes.

If women cannot speak the code without alienation and are deprived of authentic speech, the men often appear caught in a brutal network of dynastic interests and ferocious rivalries which makes the care of their fragile narcissism their supreme business. As observed here, the interests of the *moi* — an inflated ideal ego rather than a genuine ego ideal — triumph over those of the object. Unable to get in touch with their own genuine feelings, obsessed with the wiles of *'femmes habiles'* whose sometimes authentic emotions they cannot hear, they too are caught in a code without *parole* and trapped in misrecognition. Hedonism and misogyny compose their perverted ethics — unless they appear in one of the forward-looking texts which 'colonised' traditional male space with feminine values.

So these texts are not utopian or revolutionary until the modern reader teases out the implications of their warring discourses and animates with his — with *her* — gaze these virtual, holographic images. But they are refreshing, like all recovered memory, which is an excursion outside a canon built for coherence and readability . They put us in touch with the craziness of human desires, for we can read many of these works as veritable thought-experiments where alternatives are explored, in a kind of periodic table of strange, subversive episodes which legitimise the creativity of human relationships. Driven underground by inexorable social codes but preserved by the forces of fiction, the *savoir* they represent can only be recovered by the forces of critical analysis, which resuscitate not only the unthought but, as we saw, the unsayable, the unconscious of an era, and indeed of ours.

For without idealising our own time, we have seen that only the methodical conquest of human rights, especially those of women, allows for a proper reading of those texts. With the acquisition of legal rights and especially the *prise de la parole*, the complex goal of female fulfilment has not destroyed but rephrased the emotional and social ideal of happiness naively voiced by the mother of the princesse de Clèves; instead, it spreads its complexity and richness to these real and fictional lives which attempted, long before it became possible, to conceive and realise it, with all its momentous social consequences.

But just as victory can best be proved by the establishment of new, henceforth unremarkable norms, a truly post-feminist stance must mean, if the word has any meaning, that feminist ideals can be held within different contexts. This is how we can read the only chapter here which deals with a medieval text. Christine de Pizan's *Ditié de Jehanne d'Arc* may at first seem a missed opportunity to hold Joan, an outstanding instance of female achievement, as a role model. With her independence of action and her dynamism, she fulfils, for instance, the criteria listed by Marina Warner in her study of feminist heroines. Yet the author, herself a feminist icon because of the content of her works and because she earned her living exclusively from her pen, is on the contrary demonstrably keen to present Joan not only as an exceptional, almost supernatural being, but also, for all her dynamism, as a passive instrument of God's will. This is because Christine, herself a writer on politics, saw this as the best strategy for the precise political purpose she had in mind: the liberation of a whole nation rather than that of a gender. We may think of Beauvoir, who did realise in later life that the facile equation between political progressivism and progress in women's rights had to yield to more specific strategies foregrounding the latter, but who did not abandon political concerns for all that. Feminism will have truly won when it is safe and legitimate to place it among other concerns which might at times be at the top of a woman's agenda. This is not the least important facet of this many-sided and thought-provoking book.

Annette Lavers
Fielden Professor of French
UNIVERSITY COLLEGE LONDON

ROSALIND BROWN-GRANT

'Hee! Quel Honneur au Femenin Sexe!': Female heroism in Christine de Pizan's *Ditié de Jehanne d'Arc*

Feminist scholarship, since its inception, has often been concerned with cele-brating women's achievements in all areas of human endeavour. In the fields of literature and history in particular, feminist scholars have frequently hailed illustrious women authors and exceptional female figures as heroines who led fulfilling lives independent of male control.[1] For many modern critics, both those specialising in the medieval period and those working outside it, the fifteenth-century writer Christine de Pizan[2] is one such literary heroine by virtue of being the first medieval woman author we know of who earned her living exclusively from her pen.[3] Indeed, Christine has frequently been enlisted into the modern feminist cause itself because of the defence of women offered in her most famous work, the *Livre de la Cité des Dames* (1405).[4] Moreover, Christine's last work, the *Ditié de Jehanne d'Arc* (1429), composed at the end of a career spanning over three decades, is devoted to perhaps the greatest heroine in French history.[5] This example of a notable woman writer preserving for posterity the deeds of an extraordinary woman warrior would seem to com-mand an obvious place in a history of female heroism. Yet we need to ask whether the criteria by which modern feminists see historical figures such as Joan of Arc as heroines are actually appropriate for study either of Christine's medieval defence of women in general, or of her eulogy of Joan in particular.

A useful starting point for this discussion is provided by the influential analysis of Joan of Arc by Marina Warner, which is an important contribution to the study of women's place within history with a view to establishing a gallery of feminist heroines from the past.[6] Warner justifies her inclusion of the Maid of Orleans in this gallery in the following terms:

Joan of Arc is a pre-eminent heroine because she belongs to the sphere of *action*, while so many feminine figures or models are assigned and confined to the sphere of contemplation. She is anomalous in our culture, a woman re-nowned for *doing something on her own*, not by birthright. She has extended the taxonomy of female types; she makes evident the dimension of women's *dynamism*. It is urgent that this taxonomy be expanded further and that the multifarious duties that women have historically undertaken be recognized, researched and named. [...] we must develop a richer vocabulary for female activity than we use at present, with our restrictions of wife, mother, mis-tress, muse.[7]

For Warner then, Joan is a heroine according to three main criteria: her poten-tial status as a female role model, her independence of action, and her dyna-mism. Most modern feminists would probably concur with Warner in accepting these as essential criteria by which to assess whether or not a woman should be counted as a heroine. Christine de Pizan's own fervent endorsement of Joan in the *Ditié*, where she exclaims, 'Hee! Quel honneur au femenin|Sexe!' (II. 265–66), would certainly seem to echo Warner's enthusiasm for the Maid as an illustrious representative of womankind. However, I shall argue here that Christine's political purpose and rhetorical constraints in presenting Joan as a God-sent saviour meant that she constructed a model of female heroism which is in fact very different from that of Warner. In other words, conceptions of heroism, including female heroism, are historically specific in their nature and purpose.

How relevant are Warner's three criteria of heroism to Christine's repre-sentation of Joan as a heroic figure? The notion of the heroine as a role model for other women is actually the least appropriate criterion for an understanding of Christine's celebration of Joan and for her defence of women in general. Indeed, Christine's failure to prescribe her heroines as practical role models whose deeds should be emulated by other women has even caused some modern critics to question her own status as a feminist literary heroine.[8] For instance, in the *Cité des Dames*, a catalogue of famous women of the past who distinguished themselves as warriors, inventors and leaders, teachers, artists and martyrs,

Christine appears to be an heroic forerunner of modern feminism in championing those women whose actions transcended the limitations imposed on them
by their societies. However, in the sequel to the *Cité des Dames*, the *Livre des
Trois Vertus*, Christine's ambitions for her contemporaries seem to be rather
more modest since she limits her practical advice to women of her own day
simply to issues such as how to preserve their chastity, how to dress and speak
with decorum, and even how to tolerate a cruel or wayward husband.[9] Modern
readers have often been profoundly disappointed that Christine failed to advo-
cate for her contemporaries the range of activities which she applauds in her
heroines of the past.[10]

Yet reading these two texts with this expectation in mind is to misunder-
stand how Christine intended the heroines of the *Cité des Dames* to function as
role models for her medieval readership. Christine's primary aim in her defence
of women was not to propound reform of the existing social and political order
but rather to refute misogynist slanders about the sinfulness of the female sex: to
her mind, a moral attack on women had to be refuted on equally moral
grounds. The women of the *Cité des Dames* are thus mostly exceptional figures
of history whose deeds Christine certainly cites as instances of female achievement but whom she does not necessarily propose as being worthy of literal
emulation. She does not, for example, advise her readers to cut off one of their
breasts, like the Amazons, the better to shoot their bows and arrows, nor does
she encourage them to endure the tortures of martyrdom, like the virgin saints
who form the cornerstone of her book.[11] Instead, Christine enjoins her readers
to translate the virtuous moral qualities such as steadfastness, exhibited by these
exceptional individuals of the past, into terms which would be applicable to the
contemporary domain in which her readers were actually living. Indeed, even
the *Cité des Dames* itself contains a whole section devoted to heroines who were
virtuous wives, mothers, daughters and lovers and whose moral qualities, such
as discretion, mercifulness, pity and kindness, anticipate the advice that
Christine would elaborate more fully in the *Trois Vertus*. The gap between
Christine's two texts in terms of what she celebrates in women of the past and
what she advocates for women of the present thus disappears once we under-

stand the nature of her defence of women, one which was based on emulation of moral qualities rather than of literal deeds.

If Christine's fifteenth-century brand of feminism involved a radically different conception of female role models from that propounded by modern scholars, where does this leave her portrayal of Joan of Arc as heroine of the *Ditié*? Does the Maid represent, as a number of critics have maintained, the culmination of the teachings contained in the *Cité des Dames*, by providing the ultimate exemplar of female moral virtue with which to refute misogynist slanders?[12] I shall argue here that, in fact, unlike Warner, Christine does not present Joan in the *Ditié* as a role model in terms of her deeds. Nor even, as in the *Cité des Dames*, does she propose that women should emulate Joan for her moral qualities. Rather, though Christine, like Warner, stresses Joan's dynamism, she in effect rejects Warner's criterion of independence of action as a key component of heroism. Indeed, Christine ultimately subordinates her celebration of Joan as an exemplary member of the female sex to her depiction of the Maid as an atypical woman whose actions are determined by her role as instrument of God. Although to the modern mind this strategy of emphasising both Joan's dynamism and her subjection to some higher force might seem paradoxical, for Christine it was completely logical, given the very precise political purpose for which she created her text.[13]

What was Christine attempting to achieve in the *Ditié* and for whom was she writing? The text comprises 61 stanzas of octosyllabic verse which she composed at the end of July 1429, at the height of Joan's success in turning the tide in the war against England. On 8 May, Joan had raised the siege of Orleans, a town of enormous strategic importance, and, on 17 July, she had brought about the coronation of Charles VII, the disinherited king, in Rheims Cathedral. In the *Ditié*, Christine adopts a first person voice with which to address all the protagonists involved in the war with England, explicitly apostrophising Charles, Joan herself, the French army, the French rebel towns including Paris, and the English.[14] She alternates these passages of apostrophe with others of narration which outline what Joan has achieved so far and what remains to be done for the Maid to bring peace and prosperity back to the kingdom.[15] The text ends by stressing that the King is approaching Paris and that the time of an

imminent crisis of national conscience for the French people is near.[16]
Christine's aims in the *Ditié* are thus two-fold: firstly, to celebrate Joan's extraordinary deeds; and, secondly, to argue that these deeds are proof that Joan
has divine backing, which is the reason why the country should unite behind
her, acknowledge Charles as the rightful king, and expel the English.

Although modern readers are most familiar with Christine's texts in
defence of women, the *Ditié*'s focus on political concerns is, in fact, typical of
her work as a whole. In the early years of the century, she had composed numerous texts offering advice on kingship, good government, chivalry, and even
the art of warfare to her royal patrons at the Valois court.[17] She had also inter-
vened on several earlier occasions to plead for peace and to prevent civil war in
France by writing epistles to the key players in the struggle for control of the
French crown.[18] It was this long-standing interest in the well-being of her
adopted country and the political imperative of persuading the people of France
to rally to Joan's side which dictated the terms in which Christine chose to
depict her heroine.[19]

Given Christine's political aims in the *Ditié*, she presents Joan not as a
moral exemplar of female virtue, but rather as the miraculous, if unlikely instrument of God. She thus adopts four key rhetorical devices by which to represent
her heroine as France's saviour. Firstly, Christine emphasises that far from
acting on her own independent initiative, as Warner suggests, Joan's arrival on
the French political scene has been ordained by Providence and foretold by
ancient prophecy. Joan's appearance in the *Ditié* is thus delayed for eleven
stanzas in order for Christine to begin by evoking the power of Providence and
to situate the Maid's place in relation to it. Christine mentions Joan's deeds only
indirectly in these opening stanzas by referring instead to the transformations
that have occurred both in her own life and in that of Charles VII as a result of
the recent changes in France's fortunes. For Christine, it could only have been
the hand of Providence which has brought about these changes since, suddenly,
the state of deep unhappiness to which she had been reduced for the previous
eleven years, due to the desperate political situation in the country, has been
replaced by her new state of extraordinary joy. She underscores the dramatic
nature of this transformation through a series of antitheses: *'pleurer/rire'*,

'deuil/joie', 'temps sec (yvernage)/temps vert (printemps)' (stanzas I–III). The images she uses to describe the transformation brought about in Charles VII's life are even more suggestive of the workings of Providence, for, in the space of a single stanza, he is metamorphosed from being a 'degeté enfant|Du roy de France legitime' (II. 33–34) to being a 'roy coronné [...] d'esperons d'or esperonné' (II. 38–40). Christine then proceeds to acknowledge explicitly the role of Providence in these events, stating: 'Dieu a tout ce fait de sa grace' (I. 50). She thus sets the stage for presenting Joan's appearance in France's history as a miraculous event, one which she describes as 'merveillable' (I. 58) and as 'hors de toute opinion' (I. 74).

Christine goes on to emphasise the extraordinary nature of this divine intervention in France's fortunes by providing her readers with a dramatic shock: the instrument whom God has chosen in order to save France in its hour of need is no battle-hardened warrior of previous military campaigns but a mere 'vierge tendre' (I. 86), a 'simple bergiere' (I. 198). Christine declares that it is the very unlikely nature of such a saviour which proves that God's hand is at work in these human affairs. She thereby echoes the view of patriotic theologians writing about Joan at this time, such as Jean Gerson, Chancellor of the University of Paris, who quoted I Corinthians, 1. 27 to show that the Maid was part of God's divine plan to elect 'the weak things of the world to confound the things that are mighty'.[20] To both Christine's and Gerson's mind therefore, Joan's seeming powerlessness by virtue of her sex, her age and her humble social origins, attests all the more to her status as God's chosen instrument.[21]

Christine underlines Joan's role as a providential heroine by referring to numerous ancient prophecies which seemed to foretell her coming as France's God-sent saviour:

> Car Merlin et Sebile et Bede,
> Plus de Vc ans a la virent
> En esperit, et pour remede
> En France en leurs escripz la mirent,
> Et leurs prophecies en firent. (II. 241–45)

Although, to the modern mind, this invocation of prophecy might seem an unreliable means to bolster one's argument, it must be remembered that, during the course of the Hundred Years War, both the French and the English had repeatedly used prophecy foretelling eventual victory for their side as a means of justifying continuation of the conflict.[22] Indeed, as many critics have pointed out, Christine had a particular affinity for prophecy since she had already associated it with the power of women's speech in their role as advisors to kings and princes,[23] as in the figure of the Sibyls of Antiquity who occupy an important place in the *Cité des Dames*.[24] More importantly, Christine in the *Ditié* evokes these three famous prophets, Merlin, Sibyl and Bede, in order to abrogate the power of prophecy to herself and to predict what Joan will go on to accomplish in the future. Christine thus claims that not only is the Maid destined to expel the English, she will then proceed to unite all Christendom by crushing heresy, ending the Great Schism, and, most significantly of all, by leading a crusade against the Saracens with the aim of reconquering Jerusalem (stanzas XLI– XLIII). Christine sums up her belief in Joan's divine mission on earth, stating:

> Si croy que Dieu ça jus l'adonne
> Afin que paix soit par son fait. (II. 351–52)

The second rhetorical device by which Christine exalts Joan as a heroine does stress the Maid's dynamism, one of Warner's key criteria of heroism, but at the same time minimises the autonomy of her deeds. The necessity of presenting Joan as heaven-sent, in order to convince her fellow countrymen and women to accept the Maid as their saviour, leads Christine to posit a divine 'chain of command' running directly from God through Joan to Charles VII and, by extension, to the entire French people. Joan is thus shown to be passive in relation to God for whom she is an instrument, but active in relation to Charles for whose benefit she performs her extraordinary deeds.[25] Christine uses a striking number of passive verbal constructions in order to illustrate the subordination of Joan's actions to God's will, as in the following example:

> Par miracle fut envoiée
> Et divine amonition,
> De l'ange de Dieu convoiée
> Au roy, pour sa provision. (II. 225–28)

However, in order to stress the workings of this 'chain of command', Christine also uses parallel verbal constructions to show that whatever God instructs Joan to do, she must in turn instruct Charles to do. Thus, if Joan is able to recover rebel towns and castles at the head of the French army under the guidance of God 'qui la menne' (I. 288), so Charles must recover the Holy Land at the head of a crusade, under the guidance of Joan '[qui] là menra' (I. 339).[26] Similarly, if Charles shows mercy to the rebels who surrender to him, it is because Joan has been commanded by God to persuade him to do so. Moreover, in surrendering to Charles, these rebels too take up their place in the 'chain of command' as loyal subjects:

> Helas! Il est si debonnaire
> Qu'à chascun il veult pardonner!
> Et la Pucelle lui fait faire,
> Qui ensuit Dieu. Or ordonner
> Vueillez vos cueurs et vous donner
> Comme loyaulx François à lui! (II. 465–70)

The third rhetorical device adopted by Christine to laud Joan's heroism is to present the Maid's martial qualities as superlative, even supernatural. This device takes nothing away from Joan's abilities as a dynamic warrior but it does tend to militate against the possibility of taking her as a role model for other women. Christine highlights Joan's soldierly prowess by comparing her favourably to both Old Testament and pagan figures who distinguished themselves in their service to their country. She thus elevates Joan over Biblical leaders such as Moses, Joshua and Gideon (stanzas XXIII, XXV, and XXVII, respectively) and classical heroes such as Hector and Achilles (stanza XXXVI). Similarly, Christine argues that Joan is superior to Esther, Deborah and Judith, as well as to the unspecified 'preuses' or heroic women of the pagan past, whom most critics have taken to mean the Amazons (stanza XXVIII).[27] However, although Christine's patriotic male contemporaries did not hesitate to refer to Joan as a kind of Amazon herself, dubbing her a Penthesilea or a Camilla,[28] it is significant that Christine did not choose to make this comparison explicitly in the *Ditié*, despite having celebrated the deeds of the Amazons in the *Cité des Dames*.[29] On the contrary, Christine insists that Joan's ability to bear arms is truly miraculous precisely because it is beyond the innate capacity of the female sex to do so. Unlike the Amazons who were able to conquer their natural weakness by altering their bodies and training themselves to fight off invaders, Joan's extraordinary physical strength cannot be attributed to upbringing:

> Une fillete de XVI ans
> (N'est-ce pas chose fors nature?),
> Ains *semble* que sa norriture
> Y soit, tant y est fort et dure! (II. 273–77, emphasis added)

By using the verb 'sembler', Christine casts doubt on the idea of upbringing or 'norriture' as a sufficient explanation of Joan's abilities, and thus suggests a different explanation, one which she is not slow to provide: 'Mais tout ce fait Dieu, qui la menne' (I. 288).

The final rhetorical device which we need to consider is Christine's comparison of Joan with the Virgin Mary. This allusion to the most illustrious of women was not, however, intended to make Joan into any more of a female role model for contemporary readers of the *Ditié*. Rather, Christine equates Joan with a figure who, by virtue of her status as a virgin mother, is as unique and atypical as the maiden warrior herself.[30] Christine's choice of this particular device would seem to be informed by a prophecy which had gained currency around 1429 and which stated that France had been destroyed by one woman, but would be restored by another.[31] This prophecy, which clearly transposed the traditional juxtaposition of Eve as sinner and Mary as redeemer, was taken by Christine's contemporaries to refer to the downfall of the country brought about by the Queen, Isabeau de Bavière, who had claimed in 1420 that her son Charles VII was illegitimate and thus not entitled to the throne, and to the imminent restoration of France's fortunes to be brought about by Joan, the all-conquering virgin.[32] Christine echoes this prophetic association of Joan with Mary by constructing her own parallels between the two. Like the Virgin, Joan is referred to as blessed, 'beneurée' (I. 161); as having been favoured by God, 'Puis que Dieu t'a tant honnorée' (I. 163); and as having been filled with the Holy Spirit, 'En qui le Saint Esperit réa | Sa grant grace' (II. 172-73). Christine takes these parallels a stage further by invoking a tradition established since the twelfth century of soliciting the Virgin as 'a source of aid and divine intervention'.[33] She thus likens Joan to Mary as an intercessor for peace and applies to her a metaphor often used to describe the merciful Virgin: 'Qui donne à France la mamelle | De paix et doulce norriture' (II. 189-90).[34] The effect of these comparisons between Joan and Mary is therefore to stress that, whilst the Maid brings honour to her sex by her actions, she, like the Virgin, has accomplished deeds which no other woman could possibly perform without the grace of God.

Christine de Pizan's *Ditié de Jehanne d'Arc* thus demonstrates that the very notion of what constitutes a heroine is, of necessity, historically and contextually specific. Her depiction of Joan as a miraculous, even supernatural, figure clearly runs counter to the modern concept, as propounded by Marina Warner, of the heroine as a dynamic, independent role model who can motivate other women to emulate her achievements. On the contrary, Christine's rhetorical strategy is to present Joan as a salvific heroine who is utterly atypical of ordinary womankind. This strategy may seem paradoxical to late twentieth-century feminists but it was determined by political goals which were very different from our own ideological concerns. If the *Ditié* appears to be a lost opportunity for Christine to wave the flag for female liberation, it is perhaps because the project of convincing her contemporaries to put their faith in a woman as saviour of France in its darkest hour seemed to her to be a rather more urgent task.

UNIVERSITY OF LEEDS

NOTES

1. Since it would be impossible to give a full bibliography of feminist scholarship, I shall simply cite some of the most pioneering studies. In history, see Michelle Zimbalist Rosaldo and Louise Lamphere, *Women, Culture and Society* (Stanford, CA: Stanford University Press, 1974); Eileen Power, *Medieval Women*, ed. by M.M. Postan (Cambridge: Cambridge University Press, 1975); *Becoming Visible: Women in European History*, ed. by Renate Bridenthal and Claudia Koonz (Boston: Houghton Mifflin, 1977); Joan Kelly, *Women, History and Theory* (Chicago: Chicago University Press, 1984); *Women in Medieval History and Historiography*, ed. by Susan Mosher Stuard (Philadelphia: University of Pennsylvania Press, 1987). In literature, see Virginia Woolf, *A Room of One's Own* (London: Hogarth Press, 1929); Ellen Moers, *Literary Women: The Great Writers* (Garden City, NY: Doubleday, 1976); Elaine Showalter, *A Literature of Their Own: British Women Novelists from Brontë to Lessing* (Princeton: Princeton University Press, 1977); Sandra M. Gilbert and Susan Gubar, *The Madwoman in the Attic: The Woman Writer and the Nineteenth Century Imagination* (New Haven, CT: Yale University Press, 1979).

2. For standard studies of the life and works of Christine de Pizan, see Marie-Josèphe Pinet, *Christine de Pisan 1364–1430: étude biographique et littéraire*, Bibliothèque du XVe Siècle, 35 (Paris: Champion, 1927); Enid McLeod, *The Order of the Rose: The Life and Ideas of Christine de Pizan* (London: Chatto and Windus, 1976); Régine Pernoud, *Christine de Pisan* (Paris: Calmann-Lévy, 1982); Charity Cannon Willard, *Christine de Pizan: Her Life and Works* (New York: Persea Books, 1984).

3. For general overviews of Christine as a woman writer, see Léon Abensour, *Histoire générale du féminisme* (Geneva: Slatkine Reprints, 1979), pp. 135–39; (originally Paris: Delagrave, 1921); Maïté Albistur and Daniel Armogathe, *Histoire du féminisme français du Moyen Age à nos jours* (Paris: Des Femmes, 1977), pp. 53–67. For more detailed studies of Christine's place in French literary history, see Susan Groag Bell, 'Christine de Pizan (1364–1430): humanism and the problem of a studious woman', *Feminist Studies*, 3 (1976), 173–84; Leslie Altman, 'Christine de Pizan: first professional woman of letters (1364–1430?)', in *Female Scholars: A Tradition of Learned Women before 1800*, ed. by Jeanie R. Brink (Montreal: Eden Women's Publications, 1980), pp. 7–23.

4. For an edition of this text, hereafter referred to as the *Cité des Dames*, see Maureen Cheney Curnow, 'The *Livre de la Cité des Dames* of Christine de Pizan: a critical edition', 2 vols (unpublished doctoral dissertation, Vanderbilt University, 1975). For selected studies of Christine's feminism in the *Cité des Dames*, see Rose Rigaud, *Les Idées féministes de Christine de Pizan* (Neuchâtel: Attinger, 1911; Geneva: Slatkine, 1973), pp. 75–114; Sandra L. Hindman, 'With ink and mortar: Christine de Pizan's

Cité des Dames: an art essay', *Feminist Studies*, 10 (1984), 457–84; Beatrice Gottlieb, 'The problem of feminism in the fifteenth century', in *Women of the Medieval World*, ed. by Julius Kirschner and Suzanne F. Wemple (Oxford: Blackwell, 1985), pp. 337–64; Susan Schibanoff, 'Taking the gold out of Egypt: the art of reading as a woman', in *Gender and Reading: Essays on Readers, Texts and Contexts*, ed. by Elizabeth A. Flynn and Patrocinio P. Schweickart (Baltimore: Johns Hopkins University Press, 1986), pp. 83–106; Patricia A. Phillippy, 'Establishing authority: Boccaccio's *De Claris Mulieribus* and Christine de Pizan's *Cité des Dames*', *Romanic Review*, 77 (1986), 167–93; Maureen Quilligan, *The Allegory of Female Authority: Christine de Pizan's 'Cité des Dames'* (Ithaca, NY: Cornell University Press, 1991); Glenda K. McLeod, 'Poetics and antimisogynist polemics in Christine de Pizan's *Le Livre de la Cité des Dames*', in *Reinterpreting Christine de Pizan*, ed. by Earl Jeffrey Richards and others (Athens: University of Georgia Press, 1992), pp. 37–47.

5.   For an edition of the text, to which all page references will be given in the body of my paper, see Christine de Pisan, *Ditié de Jehanne d'Arc*, ed. and trans. by Angus J. Kennedy and Kenneth Varty, Medium Aevum Monographs, New Series IX (Oxford: Society for the Study of Mediaeval Languages and Literature, 1977). The text will hereafter be referred to as the *Ditié*. The bibliography on Joan is vast, hence only a selection of studies is cited here. For a concise account of Joan's life and achievements, see Georges Duby, *France in the Middle Ages 987–1460*, trans. by Juliet Vale (Oxford: Blackwell, 1991), pp. 288–97. For more detailed studies, see Ingvald Raknem, *Joan of Arc in History, Legend and Literature* (Oslo: Universitetsforlaget, 1971); Edward Lucie-Smith, *Joan of Arc* (London: Allen Lane, 1976); Michel Hérubel, *Charles VII* (Paris: Olivier Orban, 1981); *Jeanne d'Arc: une époque, un rayonnement, Colloque d'histoire médiévale, Orléans, Octobre, 1979* (Paris: Editions du CNRS, 1982); Régine Pernoud and Marie-Véronique Clin, *Jeanne d'Arc* (Paris: Fayard, 1986); Charles T. Wood, *Joan of Arc and Richard III: Sex, Saints and Government in the Middle Ages* (New York: Oxford University Press, 1988).

6.   Marina Warner, *Joan of Arc: the Image of Female Heroism* (Harmondsworth: Penguin, 1983).

7.   Warner, *Joan of Arc*, p. 28, emphasis added.

8.   For an example of a critic who revised her previously positive view of Christine's celebration of women in the *Cité des Dames* when providing a wider assessment of Christine's role as a political writer, see Sheila Delany, 'Rewriting woman good: gender and the anxiety of influence in two late-medieval texts', and '"Mothers to think back through": Who are they? The ambiguous case of Christine de Pizan', in her *Medieval Literary Politics: Shapes of Ideology* (Manchester: Manchester University Press, 1990), pp. 74–87, and pp. 88–103. See also Christine M. Reno, 'Christine de

Pizan: "at best a contradictory figure?"', and Sheila Delany, 'History, politics, and Christine studies: a polemical reply', in *Politics, Gender and Genre: The Political Theory of Christine de Pizan*, ed. by Margaret Brabant (Boulder, CO: Westview Press, 1992), pp. 171–92, and pp. 193–206, respectively.

9.   For an edition of this text, see *Le Livre des Trois Vertus*, ed. by Charity Cannon Willard and Eric Hicks, Bibliothèque du XVe siècle, 50 (Paris: Champion, 1989).

10.   However, for a more favourable appraisal of Christine's treatment of women in the *Livre des Trois Vertus*, see Marie-Thérèse Lorcin, 'Pouvoirs et contre-pouvoirs dans le *Livre des Trois Vertus*', *Revue des Langues Romanes*, 92, 2 (1988), 359–68; Margarete Zimmermann, '"Sages et prudentes mainagieres" in Christine de Pizan's *Livre des Trois Vertus*', in *Haushalt und Familie in Mittelalter und früher Neuzeit: Vorträge eines interdisziplinären Symposions vom 6.–9. Juni 1990 an der Rheinischen Friedrich Wilhelms-Universität Bonn*, ed. by Trude Ehlert (Sigmaringen: Jan Thorbecke Verlag, 1991), pp. 193–206; Josette A. Wisman, 'Aspects socio-économiques du "Livre des trois Vertus" de Christine de Pizan', *Le Moyen Français*, 30 (1992), 27–44; Marie-Thérèse Lorcin, 'Le "Livre des trois Vertus" et le "sermo ad status"', in *Une femme de Lettres au Moyen Age: Études réunies autour de Christine de Pizan*, ed. by Liliane Dulac and Bernard Ribémont (Orleans: Paradigme, 1995), pp. 139–50.

11.   Christine's male contemporary, the theologian Jacques Legrand, in his series of *sermones ad status*, points out to his female readers that they are not literally meant to imitate the behaviour of those wives who were so devoted to their husbands that they were prepared to kill themselves on learning of their spouses' deaths: see Jacques Legrand, *Archiloge Sophie, Livre des Bonnes Meurs*, ed. by Evencio Beltran, Bibliothèque du XVe siècle, 49 (Paris: Champion, 1986), p. 369:

> Et ja soit de ce que ainsi faire ne soit convenable ne necessaire, toutesvoies appert il par les dittes hystoires comment en mariage l'en doit avoir grant amour.

Also, on the question of how medieval readers might have been expected to read stories of female martyrdom, see Jocelyn Wogan-Browne, 'Saints' lives and the female reader', *Forum for Modern Language Studies*, 27,4 (1991), 314–32.

12.   See Alan P. Barr, 'Christine de Pisan's *Ditié de Jehanne d'Arc*: A feminist exemplum for the *Querelle des femmes*', *Fifteenth Century Studies*, 14 (1988), 1–12.

13.   For two excellent studies which examine the significance of the political context for Christine's treatment of Joan, see Liliane Dulac, 'Un écrit militant de Christine de Pizan: "le Ditié de Jehanne d'Arc"', in *Aspects of Female Existence: Proceedings from The St. Gertrud Symposium 'Women in the Middle Ages', Copenhagen, September 1978*,

ed. by Birte Carlé and others (Copenhagen: Gyldendal, 1980), pp. 115–34; Deborah Fraioli, 'The literary image of Joan of Arc: prior influences', *Speculum*, 56,4 (1981), 811–30. For studies of the text which adopt a similar perspective to my own, see Kevin Brownlee, 'Structures of authority in Christine de Pizan's "Ditié de Jehanne d'Arc"', in *Discourses of Authority in Medieval and Renaissance Literature*, ed. by Kevin Brownlee and Walter Stephens (Hanover: University Press of New England, 1989), pp. 131–50; François Suard, 'Christine de Pizan: "Le Ditié de Jehanne d'Arc"', in *Studies in Honor of Hans-Erich Keller: Medieval French and Occitan Literature and Romance Linguistics*, ed. by Rupert T. Pickens, Medieval Institute Publications, (Kalamazoo: Western Michigan University, 1993), pp. 247–60.

14. See Teddy Arnavielle, 'Structuration personnelle du *Ditié de Jehanne d'Arc* (1429)', *Revue des Langues Romanes*, 92 (1988), 287–93.

15. See Thérèse Ballet Lynn, 'The *Ditié de Jehanne d'Arc*: its political, feminist, and aesthetic significance', *Fifteenth Century Studies*, 1 (1978), 149–55.

16. See Harry F. Williams, 'Joan of Arc, Christine de Pizan, and Martin le Franc', *Fifteenth Century Studies*, 16 (1990), 233–37.

17. For editions of these political texts, see *Le Livre des Fais et des Bonnes Meurs du Sage Roy Charles V*, ed. by Suzanne Solente, 2 vols (Paris: Champion, 1936–40); *The 'Livre de la Paix' of Christine de Pisan: A Critical Edition with Introduction and Notes*, ed. by Charity Cannon Willard (The Hague: Mouton, 1958); *Le Livre du Corps de Policie*, ed. by Robert H. Lucas (Geneva: Droz, 1967); Christine Moneera Laennec, 'Christine "antygrafe": Authorship and Self in the Prose Works of Christine de Pizan with an Edition of B.N. ms. 603, *Le Livre des Fais d'Armes et de Chevalerie*' (unpublished doctoral dissertation, Yale University, 1989).

18. For editions of these more directly interventionist texts, see Christine de Pizan, '*The Epistle of the Prison of Human Life' with 'An Epistle to the Queen of France' and 'Lament on the Evils of the Civil War*', ed. and trans. by Josette A. Wisman, Garland Library of Medieval Literature, A21 (New York: Garland, 1984); *Christine de Pizan's 'Epistre de la prison de vie humaine'*, ed. by Angus J. Kennedy (Glasgow: the editor, distrib. Grant & Cutler, 1984); Angus J. Kennedy, 'Christine de Pizan's *Epistre à la Reine*', *Revue des Langues Romanes*, 92,2 (1988), 253–64.

19. Christine was, of course, Italian by birth, but brought to France at the age of four by her father Tommaso da Pizzano, who, in 1368, was appointed as court physician and astrologer to the French king Charles V: see Willard, *Christine de Pizan*, pp. 15–31.

20. Charles VII's court in exile in Poitiers actively sought the support of leading theologians and influential prophets as part of his propaganda efforts to legitimate Joan's and his military campaign, see Fraioli, 'The literary image of Joan of Arc'. For editions and studies of Jean Gerson's treatise in support of Joan, *De quadam puella*, see

Dom J-B Monnoyeur, *Traité de Gerson sur la Pucelle* (Paris: Picard, 1930); Dorothy Wayman, 'The Chancellor and Jeanne d'Arc, February–July, AD1429', *Franciscan Studies*, 17 (1957), 273-305; H. G. Francq, 'Jean Gerson's theological treatise and other memoirs in defence of Joan of Arc', *Revue de l'Université d'Ottawa*, 41 (1971), 58-80.

21. This similarity of opinion between Christine and Gerson on this particular aspect of Joan of Arc is not surprising in light of the fact that, almost thirty years previously, they had been close allies in their moral condemnation of Jean de Meung's *Roman de la Rose*; see Christine de Pisan, Jean Gerson, Jean de Montreuil, Gontier et Pierre Col, *Le Débat sur le Roman de la Rose*, ed. by Eric Hicks, Bibliothèque du XVᵉ Siècle, 43 (Paris: Champion, 1977).

22. See Michael Prestwich, *The Three Edwards: War and State in England, 1272-1377* (London: Weidenfeld and Nicholson, 1980), pp. 211-12; A. G. Rigg, 'John of Bridlington's Prophecy: A new look', *Speculum*, 63,3 (1988), 596-613.

23. See, for example, Sandra L. Hindman, *Christine de Pizan's 'Epistre Othéa': Painting and Politics at the Court of Charles VI* (Toronto: Pontifical Institute of Medieval Studies, 1986); Andrea Tarnowski, 'Le geste prophétique chez Christine de Pizan', in *Apogée et déclin: Actes du Colloque de l'URA 411, Provins, 1991*, ed. by Claude Thomasset and Michel Zink (Paris: Presses de l'Université de Paris-Sorbonne, 1993), pp. 225-36; Christine Moneera Laennec, 'Prophétie, interprétation et écriture dans "l'Avision Christine"', in *Une femme de Lettres*, ed. by Dulac and Ribémont, pp. 131-38.

24. On the Sibyls in the *Cité des Dames*, see Quilligan, *The Allegory of Female Authority*, pp. 105-16, pp. 125-30.

25. Indeed, Christine so emphasises Joan's role in helping Charles VII to regain the throne that she ends up denying almost all agency to the king himself. Addressing Charles directly, Christine exclaims: 'or voiz ton renon | Hault eslevé par la Pucelle' (II. 101-02); and describing Joan's part in the coronation, she states: 'N'a el le roy mené au sacre | Que tousjours tenoit par la main?' (II. 377-78).

26. This view of Charles VII as a reconqueror of Jerusalem is derived from a prophecy known as the Second Charlemagne prophecy which had been circulating in France since around 1382, and which predicted that a French monarch called Charles would become emperor and liberate the Holy Land. It was specifically applied by Christine to Charles in order to legitimate his struggle for control of the French crown; see Fraioli, 'The literary image of Joan of Arc', 827; Brownlee, 'Structures of authority', p. 276, note 14.

27. See, for example, Warner, *Joan of Arc*, p. 208; Fraioli, 'The literary image of Joan of Arc', 816.

28.   An example of such a writer is Jean de Colonne; for an edition of his short text, see
       Leopold Delisle, 'Nouveau témoignage relatif à la mission de Jeanne d'Arc', *Biblioth-
       èque de l'École des Chartes*, 99 (1938), 343–53. See also, Warner, *Joan of Arc*, p. 208.

29.   For a related study of this issue, see Deborah Fraioli, 'Why Joan of Arc never became
       an Amazon', in *Fresh Verdicts on Joan of Arc*, ed. by Bonnie Wheeler and Charles T.
       Wood, The New Middle Ages series (New York: Garland, 1996), pp. 189–204.

30.   However, ordinary medieval women, despite being unable to imitate the Virgin's
       miraculous virginity and motherhood, were encouraged in sermons to emulate her
       qualities of meekness and humility; see Marina Warner, *Alone of all her Sex: The Myth
       and Cult of the Virgin Mary* (London: Picador, 1985); S. H. Rigby, *English Society in
       the Later Middle Ages: Class, Status and Gender* (London: Macmillan, 1995), p. 251.

31.   See Fraioli, 'The literary image of Joan of Arc', 825–26, note 58.

32.   Duby, *France in the Middle Ages*, p. 289.

33.   Fraioli, 'The literary image of Joan of Arc', 820.

34.   On the use of this metaphor in relation to the Virgin, see Warner, *Alone of All her
       Sex*, pp. 194, 199.

JONATHAN MALLINSON

Writing wrongs:
Lettres portugaises and the search for an identity

The *Lettres portugaises* are a curious phenomenon. First published in 1669, these five letters were for over 250 years widely believed to be not a literary text, but the translation of genuine letters written by a nun, Mariana Alcoforado, to the treacherous French lover who has left her. It was only with the pioneering work of F. C. Green, and subsequent researches of Deloffre and Rougeot,[1] that the text was more confidently (and convincingly) attributed to Guilleragues; even now, though, some critics continue to question this attribution.[2]

Why then did the heroine of the text appear to contemporary readers to be so real? At one level it was the very intensity of her preoccupation with love. In Letter 5, she suggests that nuns are the ideal lovers, because they have all the time in the world to devote to their passion:

> [...] rien ne les empêche de penser incessamment à leur passion, elles ne sont point détournées par mille choses qui dissipent et qui occupent dans le monde. (173)

Unlike generations of self-possessed and virtuous heroines who had peopled the romances of Gomberville, La Calprenède and Scudéry in earlier decades, Mariane was clearly different, more passionate, more real. For the author of the *Réponses*, published anonymously in Grenoble as a sequel to this text, there could be little room for doubt:

> [...] l'ingénuité et la passion toute pure qui paroissoient dans les cinq Lettres portugaises, permettent à peu de gens de douter qu'elles n'aient été véritablement écrites.[3]

For other readers, this same absorption with love was seen to be a mark also of the writer's immodesty. Such a departure from the traditional moral standards of fictional characters would be further proof of her authenticity (and frailty) as a real woman. When Germont published his *Napolitain* in 1682, an epistolary novel clearly inspired by the *Lettres portugaises*, the *Mercure galant* of July implicitly drew attention to this moral weakness in the heroine which Germont's text had significantly rewritten and rectified. Passion there may still be, but this had been relocated in a context of propriety; truth had been turned into fiction:

> On achève d'imprimer un autre livre intitulé *Le Napolitain*. C'est une Histoire qui renferme plusieurs Lettres aussi passionnées que les *Lettres portugaises*. On aura peine à le croire, puisqu'on est persuadé que tout ce qui marque la plus violente passion est dans ces dernières. Cependant j'oserais vous assurer que celles qui sont dans l'histoire du Napolitain ne lui cèdent point. Toute la difference qu'il y a, c'est que Mademoiselle d'Ossanove, qui les a écrites, a pu les écrire et les envoyer, sans que les Personnes les plus scrupuleuses puissent blâmer sa conduite.

However, if contemporary readers were wont to see in Mariane a real, if arguably immoral female, committed to her love, they paradoxically lent to the heroine precisely the kind of identity and definition which, in the course of the letters, she seeks but fails to find. Indeed, far from being the simple expression of *la passion toute pure* or *la plus violente passion*, the letters explore the nature and validity of such emotions, as Mariane seeks to come to terms with her lover's departure and to clarify her feelings, her identity, her future. What kind of a heroine is she: helpless or heroic? in love or indifferent?

The text is characterised by the heroine's seemingly relentless changes of mood and style as she contemplates the change in her fortune. Such fluctuations are apparent from the beginning of the text. The opening lines express a sense of hopeless isolation and by the end of the first page she sees in her lover's absence incontrovertible evidence that she has been abandoned:

> [...] un avertissement trop sincère que me donne ma mauvaise fortune, qui a la cruauté de ne souffrir pas que je me flatte, et qui me dit à tous moments: cesse,

> cesse Mariane infortunée, de te consumer vainement, et de chercher un amant
> que tu ne verras jamais [...]. (147–48)

Soon afterwards, however, the opposite position is taken up, thus establishing
the two poles between which the letters will oscillate:

> Ne suis-je pas assez malheureuse sans me tourmenter par de faux soupçons?
> (148)

The apparently unarguable *avertissement* has become a *soupçon*, *sincère* is now
reduced to *faux*. Similar contradictions are manifold in the text. Letter 2 ends
with the words:

> Adieu, adieu, ayez pitié de moi [...]. (154)

And yet in Letter 3 she can write:

> [...] je ne veux point de votre pitié. (157)

In Letter 1, she misses the *repos* in her life when she was blissfully unaware of
his existence:

> [...] pourquoi avez-vous été si acharné à me rendre malheureuse? que ne me
> laissiez-vous en repos dans mon cloître? vous avais-je fait quelque injure? (150)

But this lament is re-written in Letter 3 when she scornfully dismisses the value
of her life before she made his acquaintance:

> [...] que ferais-je, hélas! sans tant de haine et sans tant d'amour qui remplissent
> mon cœur? Pourrais-je survivre à ce qui m'occupe incessamment, pour mener
> une vie tranquille et languissante? Ce vide et cette insensibilité ne peuvent me
> convenir. (163)

Any return to a former state would be impossible and she sees it now in quite different terms. *Repos* becomes *vide*, and if in Letter 1 she saw her present state as *malheureuse* in comparison with her former life, she now sees her earlier identity as unbearably *tranquille* and *languissante* in comparison with what she now knows and is. In both letters she compares past with present, but she does so in different ways, in different words. Even her recollection of their past together is subject to the same fluctuations. In Letter 1, the time spent with her lover is seen as a haven of bliss, now regrettably lost:

> Comment se peut-il faire que les souvenirs des moments si agréables soient devenus si cruels? et faut-il que, contre leur nature, ils ne servent qu'à tyranniser mon cœur? (148)

But the perspective changes later. What she has earlier called *moments si agréables* are seen now to have concealed a tissue of worries — about him, her love and their relationship:

> Je mourais de frayeur que vous ne me fussiez pas fidèle, je voulais vous voir à tous moments, et cela n'était pas possible, j'étais troublée par le péril que vous couriez en entrant dans ce couvent; je ne vivais pas lorsque vous étiez à l'armée, j'étais au désespoir de n'être pas plus belle et plus digne de vous, je murmurais contre la médiocrité de ma condition, je croyais souvent que l'attachement que vous paraissiez avoir pour moi vous pourrait faire quelque tort; il me semblait que je ne vous aimais pas assez, j'appréhendais pour vous la colère de mes parents, et j'étais enfin dans un état aussi pitoyable qu'est celui où je suis présentement. (173–74)

What is true of the heroine's attitudes to her lover and her past, is true also of her representation of herself. In the course of the letters, she appears in a number of familiar female guises. In Letter 2, she is forthright in her accusations of his infidelity, certain of his self-seeking nature and of her own positive response to it:

[...] la disposition que vous avez à me trahir l'emporte enfin sur la justice que vous devez à tout ce que j'ai fait pour vous. (151)[4]

Later in the same letter, static lament gives way to a more dynamic vision, and critical reproach becomes affirmation of love as she expresses the wish to follow him as a servant:

Ah! j'envie le bonheur d'Emmanuel et de Francisque; pourquoi ne suis-je pas incessamment avec vous, comme eux? je vous aurais suivi, et je vous aurais assurément servi de meilleur cœur. (153)[5]

Shortly afterwards, she is transformed again into the adoring and pitiful mistress:

[...] je sors le moins qu'il m'est possible de ma chambre, où vous êtes venu tant de fois, et je regarde sans cesse votre portrait, qui m'est mille fois plus cher que ma vie. (154)

Similar fluctuations are seen in different letters. In Letter 3, she has the voice of an outraged heroine:

J'ai bien du dépit contre moi-même, quand je fais réflexion sur tout ce que je vous ai sacrifié [...], (157)

only to move within lines to an attitude of devotion which, she will claim, more faithfully represents her authentic self:

Cependant je sens bien que mes remords ne sont pas véritables, que je voudrais du meilleur de mon cœur avoir couru pour l'amour de vous de plus grands dangers [...]. (157)

But which is her authentic self? The letters record and embody the repeated failure of her enterprise to identify attitudes which are stable, *véritables*, truly her; tone changes even as we read, even as Mariane writes. She makes

many affirmative statements about her feelings, but these are often negated by
the context. In Letter 1, she claims that she is resigned to her fate, but such a
claim comes in the middle of a lament, and can thus have no absolute force:

> [...] puis-je jamais être sans maux, tant que je ne vous verrai pas? Je les sup-
> porte cependant sans murmurer, puisqu'ils viennent de vous. Quoi? est-ce là la
> récompense que vous me donnez pour vous avoir si tendrement aimé?
> (148–49)

And in Letter 2 she moves suddenly and unpredictably from haughty scorn of
his unquestioned insensitivity to a proud claim that he will not be able to forget
her:

> [...] je n'envie point votre indifférence, et vous me faites pitié: je vous défie de
> m'oublier entièrement; je me flatte de vous avoir mis en état de n'avoir sans
> moi que des plaisirs imparfaits. (153)

Her language again draws attention to itself as she unleashes a sequence of
confident assertions which remain, nevertheless, unconnected, unargued. She
speaks of his indifference and yet she still claims to occupy his thoughts. In such
a context, her choice of verb is significantly ambiguous, *se flatter* being often
used to suggest a desire as much as conviction.

She may lay claim to self-control, but such claims are regularly deferred,
consigned to a safe future. At the end of Letter 4 she affirms her independence,
but the proof is withheld until the next letter, itself an indication of her continued, obsessive need to communicate with her lover:

> La première [*sc.* la prochaine] ne sera pas si longue, ni si importune, vous
> pourrez l'ouvrir et la lire sur l'assurance que je vous donne; il est vrai que je
> ne dois point vous parler d'une passion qui vous déplaît, et je ne vous en
> parlerai plus. (167)

In Letter 5 contradictions occur even within sentences, as protestations that she
is self-sufficient are undermined by the persistence of *vous*:

[...] je vous parle, au moins, raisonnablement une fois en ma vie. Que ma
modération vous plaira, et que vous serez content de moi! je ne veux point le
savoir, je vous ai déjà prié de ne m'écrire plus, et je vous en conjure encore.
(174)

And in Letter 3 affirmations shade subtly into questions, casting into doubt
rather than strengthening the force of earlier statements:

[...] j'ai un plaisir funeste d'avoir hasardé ma vie et mon honneur: tout ce que
j'ai de plus précieux ne devait-il pas être en votre disposition? Et ne dois-je pas
être bien aise de l'avoir employé comme j'ai fait? (157)

In Letter 4, her text becomes the location of different, self-contradictory strands
of feeling, as she recoils from the conviction that she has been abandoned for
ever:

Je suis trop assurée de mon malheur, votre procédé injuste ne me laisse pas la
moindre raison d'en douter [...]. (165)

From this categorical statement, she moves to modifications, accumulating a
series of self-deceiving possibilities, introduced ironically by another statement
of apparent certainty (*je vois bien*):

Je vois bien que vous demeurerez en France sans de grands plaisirs, avec une
entière liberté; la fatigue d'un long voyage, quelque petite bienséance, et la
crainte de ne répondre pas à mes transports vous retiennent. Ah! ne m'appré-
hendez point! Je me contenterai de vous voir de temps en temps, et de savoir
seulement que nous sommes en même lieu: mais je me flatte peut-être [...].
(165)

Conflicting currents swirl in the text: the culminating excitement of an imag-
ined reunion as *je* and *vous* meet in *nous*, leads to the dawning suspicion of
self-deception (*je me flatte*), which is itself immediately modified by a *peut-être*.
In this context of constant fluctuation, language loses all its authority and stabil-

ity, all its power to signify. Seemingly unequivocal statements are revealed to be temporary, partial, or empty, not because there is another, more stable reality from which they deviate, but because all attempts to define feelings, to interpret the past can be no more than mere snapshots of truth, momentary, coloured and informed by mood; Mariane's character is not clear and absolute, it is just the reflection of a moment, with no fixity or definition.

Her character, though, does not simply hover between different moods, each temporary but spontaneously expressed; it is seen to waver, too, between the authentic and the artificial. This fluctuation is apparent in her changing conception of the letters she writes. In Letter 4, she expresses the hope of making contact with her lover, bringing him closer to her through her words:

> Hélas! il n'est pas en mon pouvoir de m'y résoudre, il me semble que je vous parle, quand je vous écris, et que [vous] m'êtes un peu plus présent. (167)

But by the end of the letter a quite different purpose is evoked:

> [...] j'écris plus pour moi que pour vous, je ne cherche qu'à me soulager, aussi bien la longueur de ma lettre vous fera peur, vous ne la lirez point. (168)

The letter then is construed both as a dynamic act, designed to bring about change, to initiate action, and as something more passive, reflective, personal. In Letter 2 this uncertainty of function is apparent in consecutive sentences:

> [...] ne pourriez-vous pas me venir voir, et m'emmener en France? Mais je ne le mérite pas, faites tout ce qu'il vous plaira, mon amour ne dépend plus de la manière dont vous me traiterez. (154)

And in Letter 3 similar changes occur within the same interrogative form; the focus shifts significantly from *vous* to *moi*, as an ironical question leads almost inevitably to a despairing one:

N'êtes-vous pas bien malheureux, et n'avez-vous pas bien peu de délicatesse de n'avoir su profiter qu'en cette manière de mes emportements? Et comment est-il possible qu'avec tant d'amour je n'aie pu vous rendre tout à fait heureux? (156)

Mariane is not simply a passionate mistress in search of a lover, but a heroine in search of herself, an author in search of a character.

Such fluctuations further problematise the status and authority of her utterances. Do her words reflect feelings, or do they create them? Does she write for the benefit of her lover, or is this a strategy, a form of self-deception to conceal her own hopelessness? It is clear that on many occasions Mariane does attempt to create an impression of stability in her letters; even as she composes her letters, she attempts to compose herself. On occasions she resorts to traditional patterns of eloquence. Early in Letter 1 she evokes the image of a faithless lover in a long sequence of relative clauses:

[...] cesse, cesse, Mariane infortunée, de te consumer vainement, ou de chercher un amant que tu ne verras jamais; qui a passé les mers pour te fuir, qui est en France au milieu des plaisirs, qui ne pense pas un seul moment à tes douleurs, et qui te dispense de tous ces transports, desquels il ne te sait aucun gré. (148)

As she seeks to stifle the voice of passion, she tries to pin down the character of her lover, to fix him in an unchangeable linguistic mould. Alternatively, conversely, she tries anything to touch him in Letter 4, accumulating in a seemingly endless list all the attributes she can imagine which might make her worthy of pity and thus attract him back:

Mais avant que de vous engager dans une grande passion, pensez bien à l'excès de mes douleurs, à l'incertitude de mes projets, à la diversité de mes mouvements, à l'extravagance de mes lettres, à mes confiances, à mes désespoirs, à mes souhaits, à ma jalousie! (166)

On other occasions, she seeks to overlay her evident confusion with a sem-
blance of logic, using the conjunction *puisque*, either to create the impression
that she is in fact happy:

> [...] je suis plus heureuse que vous, puisque je suis plus occupée, (153)

or to suggest undeniable proof that he has never loved her, and thus provide an
unanswerable reason why she cannot now possibly love him:

> [...] il faut que vous ayez eu pour moi de l'aversion naturelle, puisque vous ne
> m'avez pas aimée éperdument. (174)

And towards the end of Letter 1, when she tries to imagine their love surviving
beyond this separation, she has recourse to the *nous* form, repeated insistently,
self-consciously, as it creates an image of togetherness:

> Il me semble qu'en nous séparant, il [*sc.* le destin] nous a fait tout le mal que
> nous pouvions craindre; il ne saurait séparer nos cœurs; l'amour, qui est plus
> puissant que lui, les a unis pour toute notre vie. (150)

Similar linguistic manipulation is apparent, too, in her images of the self.
If she fluctuates in different ways between various stereotypical female roles, she
is seen at other times to try to anchor herself, significantly, to a more stable (and
dominant) male role, assuming responsibility for what has happened, becoming
the controlling character, indeed the only character. In Letter 4 she imagines a
dialogue in which she plays the role of both lover and mistress, finding an
answer to all his excuses; in so doing she can make her lover more present, by
speaking his words for him, but she can also adopt a more active, defining role
in a situation where she has hitherto been passive:

> [...] vous avez voulu profiter des prétextes que vous avez trouvés de retourner
> en France; un vaisseau partait: que ne le laissiez-vous partir? Votre famille
> vous avait écrit: ne savez-vous pas toutes les persécutions que j'ai souffertes de
> la mienne? Votre honneur vous engageait à m'abandonner: ai-je pris quelque

soin du mien? Vous étiez obligé d'aller servir votre roi: si tout ce qu'on dit de
lui est vrai, il n'a aucun besoin de votre secours, et il vous aurait excusé. (162)

In other places, she assumes vocabulary associated with him. If he is seen in
Letter 1 as:

[...] résolu à un éloignement qui m'est si insupportable, (147)

she takes on the same resolve:

[...] je suis résolue à vous adorer toute ma vie. (149)

Thus she puts herself on an equal footing with her lover, like him determined
and decisive.

This same approach is suggested in her use of the term *abandonner* in
Letter 2. By taking over this verb, she takes over his guilt, and preserves the
purity of his love; but she also creates for herself a more positive identity, able
to account for and control the events:

J'attribue tout ce malheur à l'aveuglement avec lequel je me suis abandonnée à
m'attacher à vous [...]. (151)

In Letter 3 she even takes upon herself the role of betrayer: if she can be apart
from her love, she argues, and still live, then *she* has deceived *him*. By reversing
their traditional roles she can express the words of a contrite lover which she so
wishes to hear and, once again, take over the initiative, and exact revenge on the
lover who has betrayed her:

Je vous ai vu partir, je ne puis espérer de vous voir jamais de retour, et je
respire cependant: je vous ai trahi, je vous en demande pardon. (157–78)

And later, in Letter 5, she tries to turn his silence into the result of her will,
requesting him no longer to write to her:

> Cependant, si tout ce que j'ai fait pour vous peut mériter que vous ayez quel-
> ques petits égards pour les grâces que je vous demande, je vous conjure de ne
> m'écrire plus, et de m'aider à vous oublier entièrement. (171)

By attributing to herself through these linguistic means a measure of
control over the past and over her lover, Mariane may appear to right the
wrongs done to her, to reaffirm herself. And yet, in different ways, it becomes
clear that language is inadequate to fulfil this function. In Letter 1, she tells her
lover that she cannot find *un nom assez funeste* (147) to describe his absence from
her, and in Letter 2 she suggests that her emotions cannot be captured in words;
to do so is to distort them:

> Il me semble que je fais le plus grand tort du monde aux sentiments de mon
> cœur, de tâcher de vous les faire connaître en les écrivant [...]. (151)

Within this spiral of spontaneity and calculation, of confidence and insecurity
which inform her letters, there are moments too of insight into the futility of
her attempt to identify and understand herself. In Letter 1, she may see herself
as the perfect mistress, for whom separation from her beloved is tantamount to
separation from life itself:

> [...] les miens [*sc.* mes yeux] sont privés de la seule lumière qui les animait.
> (147)

And yet she is forced to recognise that the truth is rather different. Such language is seen to be empty metaphor, misleading, creating a persona more stable
and ideal than she is. She had fainted at the realisation of his absence, but, to her
dismay, had subsequently regained consciousness:

> [...] je me défendis de revenir à une vie que je dois perdre pour vous [...]; je
> revis enfin, malgré moi, la lumière, je me flattais de sentir que je mourais
> d'amour. (148)

Indeed, there are moments when Mariane realises that her different emotions are not so much expressed, but are perhaps even created by the words on the page. What she feels, or is, slips away from the letters and she is left with words which express at best what she was, and at worst merely what she might wish to be:

> Il me semble même que je ne suis guère contente ni de mes douleurs, ni de l'excès de mon amour, quoique je ne puisse, hélas! me flatter assez pour être contente de vous. Je vis, infidèle que je suis, et je fais autant de choses pour conserver ma vie que pour la perdre. Ah! j'en meurs de honte: mon désespoir n'est donc que dans mes lettres? Si je vous aimais autant que je vous l'ai dit mille fois, ne serais-je pas morte il y a longtemps? (157)

She confronts now the emptiness of her own language, of her own self-image just as earlier she had suspected it in her lover's. It is not just a question of deceit, but of the unbridgeable gap between language and feelings. The feelings conveyed in her letters — of independence, of continued love, of despair — are all, in their different ways, flawed, partial, impermanent. She cannot find the identity she seeks which might give sense to her feelings and coherence to her character. She has no power to right wrongs in her actions; she achieves little in writing them in words. As she subsequently longs to die, she recognises that such longing is not *véritable*:

> Et je vous conjure de me donner ce secours, afin que je surmonte la faiblesse de mon sexe, et que je finisse toutes mes irrésolutions par un véritable désespoir [...]. (158)

Again she implicitly compares herself with heroines of fiction and legend, but finds herself wanting. They have heroic resolve, and the strength to act — and to die — for their love, while she is irresolute and weak; they suffer in reality, but she only in words. In the end, she will be reduced to silence.

It was the distinctive, fluctuating style of the *Lettres portugaises* which for many contemporary readers confirmed the authenticity of the text. In de Villiers's *Entretiens sur les Contes de fées*,[6] a speaker suggested that the letters must be genuine, because they recalled not the formal letters in fiction, but other, seemingly authentic texts — like the letters of Héloïse:

> [...] nous n'avons guère de meilleurs Ouvrages que ceux qui ont été écrits par des Auteurs véritablement touchez des passions qu'ils vouloient exprimer; c'est ce qui a rendu si excellentes les lettres d'Heloïse, les Lettres portugaises. (179)

For some, such linguistic fluidity could only be explained or 'excused' if the text were genuine — it did not otherwise merit wide attention, since it did not obey literary rules or conform to expected or accepted standards. Indeed, it was sometimes judged to be simply 'bad' writing: one speaker in Guéret's *Promenade de Saint-Cloud* was very clear on this subject:

> D'ailleurs, il n'y a pas même de stile, la plupart des périodes y sont sans mesure, et ce que j'y trouve de plus ennuyeux, ce sont de continuelles répétitions qui rebattent ce qui méritoit à peine d'être dit une seule fois.[7]

For many, though, formal patterns of rhetoric were seen to be a quite inadequate mode of expression, suggesting an inappropriate degree of intellectual control. A more authentic language of passion was seen to have its own principles of irregularity, as du Plaisir would argue; such a style does not *represent* passion, it *is* passion:

> Qu'on se plaigne et qu'on remercie en même temps, qu'on craigne et qu'on espère, qu'on prie et qu'on menace, enfin que l'on ne se connaisse plus, tous ces désordres sont des beautés, pourvu qu'ils soient exprimés naïvement; mais surtout on accommode l'expression à la vitesse de la pensée. Le langage du cœur se précipite et quand l'expression ne vole pas, elle languit.[8]

Such a view would be expressed, too, by Mme de Villedieu who, in her *Alcidamie*, focused on the rhetorical *désordres* appropriate to the depiction of love:

> On a tant de désordre dans l'esprit quand on est en cet estat, qu'il est impossi-
> ble d'éviter que les lettres ne s'en ressentent.[9]

This kind of discourse was widely held, significantly, to be distinctly feminine. In Bussy-Rabutin's *Histoire amoureuse des gaules*, Ardélise reproached her lover Candole for the inadequate, artificial and unconvincing style of his expression of love:

> D'ordinaire les grandes passions s'expliquent plus confusément, et il semble
> que vous écriviez comme un homme qui a bien de l'esprit, et qui n'est point
> amoureux, mais qui veut le faire croire.[10]

And Cotin would introduce his *Œuvres galantes* with this unequivocal praise of women writers, unparalleled in their skill at depicting passion in words:

> C'est à ces belles & à ces heureuses mains que la gloire appartient de bien
> representer les pensées du cœur; c'est à elles que la nature a donné d'exprimer
> sans affectation & sans art les sentimens de la nature.[11]

For contemporary readers, Mariane appeared to be a living figure because she was different, because she spoke this new and seemingly more authentic language, and did so in a form, the letter, which had its roots in reality. But Mariane is real, and different, in another way too. She is different from other fictional characters because she is no longer the supremely self-possessed heroine of traditional romance, confident in her love or in her anger; she is denied both the freedom to act — she is trapped in a convent — and the ability to make an impact through her letters - they receive no reply. But she is different above all, because she is different from herself, no longer sure of her identity, failing to find any stability in traditional female roles of faithful mistress, avenging fury, detached writer. The notion of consistency in character, which had been one of the principal rules of all literary composition in the classical age, is here explored and modified, as Mariane constantly shifts in her attitude to herself, her love and her lover. Different voices interact and blend in the course of the letters, with the result that the reader, like the heroine herself, can no longer tell what is created and what is spontaneous, what is real and what is role. Ironically, or perhaps appropriately, the very possibility that she may be trying vainly to create an identity for herself even as she writes, that beneath truth there may lie fiction, is one which many subsequent generations of readers found so difficult to accept.

TRINITY COLLEGE, OXFORD

NOTES

1.   F. C. Green, 'Who was the author of the *Lettres portugaises?*', *Modern Language Review*, 21 (1926), 159–67; F. Deloffre & J. Rougeot, *Lettres portugaises, Valentins et autres œuvres de Guilleragues* (Paris: Garnier, 1962). All references to the text are to the revised version of the above edition: *Chansons et bons mots, Valentins, Lettres portugaises*, Textes Littéraires Français (Geneva: Droz, 1972).

2.   Cf. Anne-Marie Clin-Lalande, Introduction to *Lettres portugaises et suites*, Livre de Poche Classique (Paris: Librairie Générale Française, 1993).

3.   A.-M. Clin-Lalande, *Lettres portugaises et suites*, p.167.

4.   Such laments by a deserted mistress are common in earlier traditions of fiction. Cf Cerinthe in Gomberville's *Carithée* (Paris: P. Billaine, 1621):

> Quoy? Toutes les obligations que tu m'as, toute l'affection que je t'ay portée,
> & tous les tourmens que j'endure pour t'aymer, ne peuvent-ils pas esmouvoir
> ton cœur perfide à me donner le foible contentement que je te demande?
> (364)

5.   This role is often found in Spanish tales. Cf. *Les Deux Pucelles* in V. d'Audiguier, *Six Nouvelles de Michel Cervantes* (Paris: J. Richer, 1621), in which Theodose dons male disguise as she goes in search of her lover.

6.   P. de Villiers, *Entretiens sur les contes de fées, et sur quelques autres ouvrages du temps* (Paris: J. Collombat, 1699).

7.   G. Guéret, *La Promenade de Saint-Cloud* (1669), ed. by G. Monval (Paris: Librairie des Bibliophiles, 1888), p. 37.

8. Du Plaisir, *Sentiments sur les lettres et sur l'histoire, avec des scrupules sur le style* (1683), ed. by P. Hourcade, Textes Littéraires Français (Genève: Droz, 1975), p. 33.

9. Mme de Villedieu, *Alcidamie* (Paris: C. de Sercey, 1661), II, 3.

10. Bussy-Rabutin, *Histoire amoureuse des gaules* (1665), ed. by J. & R. Duchêne, Folio (Paris: Gallimard, 1993) p. 32. Cf. also B. de Bonnecourse, *La Montre* (Paris: C. Barbin, 1666), in which the heroine instructs Damon about the kind of letter she wishes to receive from him:

> Mais je ne prétens pas exiger de vous de ces billets galants qui ne sont remplis que de belles pensées; je veux seulement que les vostres soient tendres, amoureux, & passionnez; & j'ayme mieux y voir beaucoup d'amour que beaucoup d'esprit. (33–34)

11. C. Cotin, *Œuvres galantes en prose & en vers* (Paris: E. Loyson, 1663).

MICHAEL MORIARTY

Decision, desire, and asymmetry in *La Princesse de Clèves*

The Princess's dilemma, on the death of her husband, has not merely an ethical but an epistemological dimension. As well as asking 'Would it be right to marry Nemours?', she is in effect asking herself whether it would be prudent so to do (the mark of a prudent person, according to Aristotle, being the ability to deliberate well about what is good or advantageous to oneself, as a means to the good life in general).[1] The question is, what kind of evidence is relevant to her deliberations?

One might query the whole notion of deliberation, asserting that the rejection of Nemours is prompted essentially by unconscious factors (fear of life, sexual repression, a residual pre-Œdipal attachment to her mother). Yet the Princess does put forward reasons for her decision, reasons of prudence as well as of duty: only if these seemed distorted or manifestly flimsy would we be compelled to interpret them as mere rationalisations. John Campbell's fine recent study argues that there is plenty of material in the text to support the view that in turning her back on passion the heroine is exercising 'a perfectly legitimate right to self-protection':[2] for not only the heroine's but other characters' experience bear out the view of passion as an alienating and destructive force. Of course, this does not necessitate the Princess's choice, since one might decide that, for all that passion makes one unhappy, it is worthwhile for its very intensity. What it does imply is that, if one values one's peace of mind, one will attempt to avoid passion.

Yet there is still a hitch, as will appear if we draw further on Aristotle's conception of prudence. Prudence is distinguished from scientific knowledge in that matters of conduct admit of variation, matters of scientific knowledge not: knowledge is of that which is universally true (*Nicomachean Ethics*, VI.5.3 (1140a–b)). Prudence, therefore, involves knowledge of particular facts, as well as general truths, since action deals with particular things (VI.7.7 (1141b)). In this case, the Princess would have to know about Nemours as well as knowing about passion in general. But there is more. That which generally happens, as regards things that can be other than they are, is the probable (*to eikos*).[3] Now one of the seventeenth-century equivalents for this term is *le vraisemblable*; and, as critics have abundantly demonstrated, *La Princesse de Clèves* puts under pressure the whole category of the *vraisemblable* (a textual feature linked, Nancy Miller suggests, to the gender of its author).[4] In other words, since the Princess is capable of performing an action 'sans exemple', might it be that she is capable of arousing a passion 'sans exemple', that is to say, one that will be durable and conducive to lasting happiness: an exception to the general rule? To bet on this possibility would be to cut oneself adrift from the general knowledge that founds the judgment of prudence (in this case, that passion leads to unhappiness). Yet it might not be imprudent, provided that one had either some particular knowledge (for instance of Nemours), in the light of which the general rule could be suspended, or a deeper understanding of passion in the light of which one could see both why it generally leads to unhappiness and why it would not, or might not, do so in this particular case.[5] To judge by her decision the Princess never obtains any such knowledge or understanding. The question is then whether the text as a whole suggests any possible grounds for an exception to the general rule.

The text constantly presents us with the figure of the unique, the superlative.[6] Many critics have subtly argued that by the abundance of superlatives it then proceeds to evacuate its own discourse. For if everyone is superlative, no-one is.[7] The rhetoric of distinction, of elevation, serves merely to level out. The effect of this is to reduce everyone to the level at which generalisations like those put forward by Mme de Chartres come fully into play.

But the text cannot dictate that we read in this way. For we might still opt to read the superlatives referentially, as a desperate attempt to do justice to a world surpassing the reader's experience (some critics have argued that the text solicits nostalgia for an older nobiliary order).[8] One reason why we might be susceptible to arguments undermining the superlatives is that we are chary of falling into such nostalgia, such *naïveté*.

Yet one should at least entertain the possibility of taking the superlatives seriously. Think of a gathering (somehow in this case it would have to be a gathering of men) discussing the greatest pop song, or the greatest cricket or football or baseball team, of all time. Clearly, their conversation might well appear absurd: pure self-generating discourse, without the slightest relationship to reality.[9] Yet to the participants what they are saying matters, and the considerations they invoke may well be pertinent within the field in question: 'Statistics, man, you're ignoring the statistics!', '[...] simply isn't England material, old man', to quote Joan Smith's cricket-loving dons.[10]

The word 'field' inevitably conjures up the work of Pierre Bourdieu. It would not be difficult to show how the court corresponds to his definition of this term as a network of objective relationships between positions: or how, corresponding to the field of the court, there is a set of behaviour-patterns and evaluations, what he would term a *habitus*.[11]

But the point is not, for the moment to investigate court behaviour-patterns and relationships, so much as to draw attention to the relationship Bourdieu establishes between the concept of *champ* and that of *illusio*: that is, in keeping with the etymological sense, involvement in the game, acceptance of the values implicit within it, recognition of the differences that count within it:

> Chaque champ produit sa forme spécifique d'*illusio*, au sens d'investissement dans le jeu qui arrache les agents à l'indifférence et les incline et les dispose à opérer les distinctions pertinentes du point de vue de la logique du champ, à distinguer ce qui est important ('ce qui m'importe', *interest*) par opposition à 'ce qui m'est *égal*', *in-différent*) du point de vue de la loi fondamentale du champ.[12]

To read the presentation of the court referentially, as a serious attempt to discriminate between possessors of outstanding qualities, is thus to participate in the *illusio* of court culture, within which these differences matter; to put oneself in the company of the seventeenth-century readership to whom such discriminations also matter, because the qualities are ones they too recognize. If we are not participants, even imaginative participants, in the courtly game, the court will inevitably appear to us as pure appearance, its discourse purely illusory in the negative epistemological sense. Here the sceptical reading of the superlatives comes into play, and can indeed be reinforced by a sober reflexion on the way the characters behave: the 'prudent' M. de Clèves making a disastrous marriage and almost literally dying of his rash interpretation of his wife's conduct, the brave and gallant Vidame de Chartres betraying his lovers and his Queen. But the point remains: if we were involved in the field, we would not feel like that; we would be under the influence of the *illusio*. The Princess's problem is to define her position in relation to the field, into which she has been inserted, not personally by her mother, but by her noble birth (which is such that *not* to present her at court would require explanation), and in which she has been kept by her marriage.

Let us thus assume that, from within the field, the narrator's attempts to present, and to discriminate between, the various courtiers will be taken seriously, and therefore that Nemours's special position has to be taken into account. The question then is whether the qualities he possesses to a superlative extent offer any reason for judging whether the Princess's love for him is likely to conduce to her happiness or to her misery.

Now another of the indeterminacies of the novel consists in the representation of the origin of love. For it is presented both as perfectly arbitrary and as highly motivated.

> Je tenais à Mme de Thémines par une inclination naturelle que je ne pouvais vaincre,

says the Vidame, and then

> comme les sentiments que j'ai pour elle [*sc.* the Queen] ne sont pas d'une nature à me rendre incapable de tout autre attachement et que l'on n'est pas amoureux par sa volonté, je le suis devenu de Mme de Martigues.[13]

There is an implication here that passion can sometimes render the lover incapable of straying: the Vidame has also referred to Mme de Thémines as 'une des plus estimables femmes du monde' (314), but the dominant suggestion is that love comes and goes rather at random: as Marivaux's Silvia puts it,

> Lorsque je l'ai aimé, c'était un amour qui m'était venu; à cette heure je ne l'aime plus, c'est un amour qui s'en va; il est venu sans mon avis, il s'en retourne de même.[14]

Another case in point is Henry VIII's passion for Anne de Boulen, which is quickly supplanted by his feelings for Jeanne Seymour (300–01). But perhaps this kind of change only occurs if you are Henry VIII or the Vidame de Chartres. In other words, we do not know how to gauge the relative contribution, to any given passionate state, of the individual nature of the lover.

This arbitrariness of passion has the obvious implication that feelings are not under the subject's control. Hence the narrator's correction of the misconception implied in the heroine's remorse: 'elle se faisait un crime de n'avoir pas eu de la passion pour lui, comme si c'eût été une chose qui eût été en son pouvoir' (377–78). But nor can such arbitrary states be counted on to subsist indefinitely. That they can be disastrous is apparent enough from the fate of the Vidame, and from the sufferings his behaviour causes Mme de Thémines (as the letter makes clear (308–10)).

The famous comment on Mme de Chartres's attitude to her daughter's betrothed slightly complicates this picture: 'elle ne craignit point de donner à sa fille un mary qu'elle ne pût aimer en lui donnant le prince de Clèves' (258).[15] As many critics have noted, the remark is ambiguous: it can mean, with an implied criticism of the mother, 'She was imprudent enough to give her daughter a husband, the Prince de Clèves, whom she simply could not love' (love being arbitrary and not in one's power). If love means something different here, something other than this arbitrary and unpredictable urge, then the implication is rather that 'She had no fear that in giving her daughter the Prince de Clèves she was giving her a husband she could not love': that is, a husband for any reason fundamentally unlovable.[16] But the point would still remain that passion as such is arbitrary and unreliable. If this were generally true, then the

Princess would indeed be prudent to refrain from committing herself to her feelings for Nemours and to his for her.

Henri's attachment for Mme de Valentinois appears in part to contradict this picture. The heroine finds it incomprehensible, given that the King's mistress is older than he and unfaithful to him (264). Is it then that passion is simply mysterious, there being no reason why it should arise, or survive, but no reason either why it should fade? What Mme de Chartres says, though, is slightly different: that his attachment is *inexcusable* (but if an attachment is excusable, there must be some reason for it); and she tacitly implies that it is *comprehensible* as the result of the impact of Mme de Valentinois's seductions on an immature youth (264, 266). So the story of Henri and Mme de Valentinois suggests that behind the apparent arbitrariness of passion there is a certain intelligibility, a degree of motivation.

When M. de Clèves sees the heroine in the jeweller's shop,

> il demeura si touché de sa beauté et de l'air modeste qu'il avait remarqué dans ses actions qu'on peut dire qu'il conçut pour elle dès ce moment une passion et une estime extraordinaires. (249)

And he is

> si rempli de l'esprit et de la beauté de Mlle de Chartres qu'il ne pouvait parler d'autre chose. (250)

Perhaps passion is motivated by beauty and esteem by modesty and *esprit*: in any case, esteem here reinforces passion. Valincour's comment, however, is typically acute: what actions, exactly, has the Prince seen Mlle de Chartres carry out, what proofs of her *esprit* has she given?[17] This is unfair, of course: her modesty appears in her blushing and in her leaving the shop rather promptly, her *esprit* in the self-possession with which she ignores the Prince's attentions while paying due respect to his rank. What Valincour's comments do show, however, is the possibility, for which he opts, of reading the Princess' passion as arbitrary, as underdetermined, from a discourse that appears to motivate it.

In general, however, there are clearer signs that passion is less arbitrary than it may appear:

> Ce prince [Nemours] était fait d'une sorte qu'il était difficile de n'être pas surprise de le voir quand on ne l'avait jamais vu [...]; mais il était difficile aussi de voir Mme de Clèves pour la première fois sans avoir un grand étonnement. (261–62)

Although the form of the adjective 'surprise' (criticized by Valincour (p. 237)) shows these reactions, or at least that of the Princess, as gendered, the narrator presents them as in some sense typical, and also as complementary. And this complementarity is accentuated by a later comment of the narrator's: 'se voyant l'un et l'autre ce qu'il y avait de plus parfait à la cour, il était difficile qu'ils ne se plussent infiniment' (263). This kind of reciprocity had of course been prepared for by the King's enjoining the Princess to dance with Nemours, and by the court's admiration when they dance together (261, 262).[18]

At this level, the narrator's initial portrait gallery, if we retain the option of taking it seriously, assumes its full importance. The court appears almost as a sort of machine for the organization, and even the production, of desire, in that all its occupations tend towards that end (and to intertwined political ends: 'l'Amour était toujours mêlé aux affaires et les affaires à l'Amour' (252)). Firstly, the court is a collection of 'belles personnes' and 'hommes admirablement bien faits' (242). Within this framework, the capacity to arouse desire, in appropriate individuals, is valued as an index of one's own distinctive personal worth, preventing it being swamped in the pervasive excellence.[19] (The characters are existentially jeopardised - 'how can I expect to be noticed when everyone is so remarkable?' in rather the same way as the reader's judgment is textually jeopardised - 'how seriously am I supposed to take this discourse of universal excellence?') The valorisation of looks enforces the valorisation of desire. Not that desire is solely determined by looks: there is *esprit*, which compensates the Prince de Condé for his physical shortcomings (243), and there are the various physical exercises in which the courtiers excel. These latter have a specific relation to desire in that they are purely male activities: or rather, they form collective rituals (everyone can be involved) that constitute men and women as different (men perform, women look on; as when all the ladies come to watch the King playing tennis with Nemours, the Chevalier de Guise, and the Vidame (305)).[20] Men then are vulnerable in a sense: they may be seen to be defeated in the competition, but this individual vulnerability is a sacrifice they collectively make in return for the power to compel the female gaze. *Esprit*, too, has its rituals: for it is manifested above all in conversation, an activity in which both sexes participate. More precisely, we see groups of women conversing together, like the circle of the Reine Dauphine (271, 275), and also mixed groups, like the Queen's circle (242). But an all-woman gathering can be changed into a mixed one by the arrival of a man of sufficient rank to claim entry, like the Prince de Condé (271).[21] In other words, the court combines two kinds of collective ritual, each involving men and women: there are those that make men compete for women's attention, like the tournament, and those that bring them together, like the conversational circle and the ball. It is the articulation between the two types that counts, for it means that the woman's perception of the man as competing against other men in a male activity is complemented, reinforced, or modified, by the experience of participating alongside him in a group conversation or dancing opposite him at a ball (the only contexts in which men see women perform).

The point of the above is not, so to speak, to protest at a gendered inequity ('tennis tournaments for women too!'), but to note how the culture serves to organise and produce desire, because the qualities it systematically displays are those that it also regards as fostering sexual desire. This is where the uniqueness of Nemours deploys its full significance.

> Ce qui le mettait au-dessus des autres était une valeur incomparable, et un agrément dans son esprit, dans son visage et dans ses actions, que l'on n'a jamais vu qu'à lui seul; il avait un enjouement qui plaisait également aux hommes et aux femmes, une adresse extraordinaire dans tous ses exercices, une manière de s'habiller qui était toujours suivie de tout le monde, sans pouvoir être imitée, et enfin un air dans toute sa personne qui faisait qu'on ne pouvait regarder que lui dans tous les lieux où il paroissait. (243-44)

Complementary, though how sketchy in comparison, is the portrayal of the heroine as unique:

> La blancheur de son teint et ses cheveux blonds lui donnaient un éclat que l'on n'a jamais vu qu'à elle. (248)

When looking is so closely related in this novel to desire, the Duke's desirability follows from his visibility:

> Il n'y avait aucune dame dans la cour dont la gloire n'eût été flattée de le voir attaché à elle; peu de celles à qui il s'était attaché, se pouvaient vanter de lui avoir résisté, et même plusieurs à qui il n'avait point témoigné de passion, n'avaient pas laissé d'en avoir pour lui. (244)

Here then desire seems anything but arbitrary: he is most desirable who most fulfils all the criteria of masculine excellence. Generally accepted criteria: women are not individualised or even categorised by their preference of one set of qualities to the exclusion of others. Thus, to be recognised as excellent, men must compete for women's desire in general: they compete for a particular woman insofar as she can perform the generic female function of certifying masculine merit. It is not that individual men happen to compete for the desire of an individual woman whose personal desiderata both might be capable of fulfilling. As J.-M. Delacomptée astutely observes:

> les hommes ne sont pas rivaux parce qu'ils convoitent les mêmes femmes, il les convoitent parce qu'ils sont rivaux: les rivalités precedent leurs objets.[22]

There seem to be no tacit rules excluding certain categories of object from the sexual competition:

> La consideration d'un mari n'empêche pas que l'on soit amoureux de sa femme. On doit haïr ceux qui le sont et non pas s'en plaindre. (334)

(Although Sancerre admits that if he had told Estouteville of his love for Mme de Tournon, his friend might have left her alone (288).)[23] Secondly, if love were purely arbitrary, or simply a matter of finding someone to one's own liking, then competition would be diffused and defused because it would not always be focused on the same objects, those of avowed superiority according to the courtly scheme of values. As it is, men's relations with one another are constantly tinged with fear of rivalry: even Nemours is afraid of Saint-André (274), as M. de Clèves is afraid of Nemours (342).

The logical consequence of this view of desire would be rather uncomfortable: for it would be that Nemours should be loved by all the women of the court, successively or simultaneously, leaving his fellow-men to the role of wallflowers, or at best fall-back options for the disappointed or discarded (Ralph Albanese refers to the other courtiers as 'des Nemours ratés').[24] This might seem a ridiculous idea, the result of being over logical about something as illogical as passion. Actually, it is voiced within the text: when the Prince de Condé is explaining Nemours's view that a lover should be happy to see his mistress at a ball where he is the host, as he was on one occasion the previous year, the Reine Dauphine comments:

> M. de Nemours avait raison [...] d'approuver que sa maîtresse allât au bal. Il y avait alors un si grand nombre de femmes à qui il donnait cette qualité que, si elles n'y fussent point venues, il y aurait eu peu de monde. (272)

This is of course a joke, and perhaps tinged with pique, but its presence does highlight a problematic area in the text. Not just Nemours's promiscuity but the disruptive influence within a system of an individual who fulfils too many of the system's criteria of excellence, leaving no room for anyone else. The arbitrariness of passion noted elsewhere serves as an antidote to the danger of the court's becoming, as a result of motivated passion, a sort of Nemours harem. Of course, this motivation could work the other way: and though the Princess is not long enough at court to equal Nemours's total of captured hearts, her bag is all the more impressive for being involuntarily acquired: M. de Clèves, the Chevalier de Guise, the Maréchal de Saint-André, not to mention the 'plusieurs autres' who are, like Saint-André 'touché[s] de sa beauté', but inhibited by her bearing from making advances to her (260).

Motivated passion thus appears as no less disruptive than arbitrary passion. But the disruption might be averted were the disruptive influences to be balanced by a complementary force: the perfect gentleman to be matched by the perfect lady. A woman perfectly complementary to Nemours would take him out of circulation, to the great relief of other men; while no other man would dare challenge him his possession of the unique. Indeed, such a woman would rescue Nemours from his one imperfection, his promiscuity, a shortcoming not from the point of view of an irrelevant Christian or humanist morality but from the courtly ethic for which the Reine Dauphine speaks: before his return from Brussels (before seeing Mme de Clèves, that is)

> il avait un nombre infini de maîtresses, et c'était même un défaut en lui; car il ménageait également celles qui avaient du mérite et celles qui n'en avaient pas. (275–76)[25]

This lack of discrimination would surely be effaced by his attachment to an object that would entirely match his own qualities and demands. And indeed Nemours does appear to be entirely changed in this way by his passion for the Princess: 'Depuis qu'il est revenu, il ne connaît ni les unes ni les autres, il n'y a jamais eu un si grand changement' (276; cf. 269).[26]

All this could be summed up as follows: within the total text of *La Princesse de Clèves*, there is a romance sub-text, which depicts the turbid agitations of the court being clarified by a moment of vision in which the epitome of masculine distinction and the epitome of female distinction confront each other, set above, but not severed from, the rest of their world by their very perfection, and brought together by their complementarity. Unless we are aware of this image, and susceptible to its charm, the full pathos of the ending can hardly come through. The question is of course whether we, and the Princess, can adhere to it.

There are two questions. How full is this complementarity? What is its relation to desire?

So far we have discussed the notion of 'motivated' passion: passion presented not as a random occurrence or the inevitable manifestation of an inflammable temperament, but as referable to some distinctive quality of its object. But these qualities are not the same thing as the object of desire, even if they are its occasion: for they might be perceived and appreciated in the mode of disinterested admiration (what the Reine Dauphine feels for the heroine's beauty (273), unless we opt to read this as a homoerotic subtext). So the question is why these qualities should arouse love as such. What is it, to quote Blake, that men in women do require (and women in men, and is it the same?).

It may seem rather naive to ask such questions, and to analyse the representation of love in a text partakes somewhat of the art of the totally obvious. However, examining even connexions that appear self-evident is salutary, as Barthes points out:[27] although one might feel that this or that textual connexion is just like life, life did not determine the necessity of the connexion in the text, not to mention, again, the point that *La Princesse de Clèves* was in its time perceived as anything but *vraisemblable*.

Given the almost inevitable causal connexion between passion and unhappiness pointed to by Campbell, it is paradoxical that passion should so often be described in terms of joy:

> M. de Nemours [...] ne [pouvait] soutenir en public la joie d'avoir un portrait de Mme de Clèves. Il sentait tout ce que la passion peut faire sentir de plus agréable. (303)

Intense pleasure again is his reaction, or part of his reaction, when she receives him coldly after the letter incident (324), and after hearing the confession (337); when he thinks back on what he has seen in the *pavillon* at Coulommiers (368); when she avows her feelings to him (384). Joy has an aphrodisiac effect: 'la joye de ce qu'il croyait avoir vu, lui donnait un air qui augmentait encore son agrément' (93); this, and its contagiousness, are nowhere clearer than in the forgery episode:

> Elle ne sentait que le plaisir de voir M. de Nemours, elle en avait une joie pure
> et sans mélange qu'elle n'avait jamais sentie: cette joie lui donnait une liberté
> et un enjouement dans l'esprit que M. de Nemours ne lui avait jamais vue et
> qui redoublait son amour. (328)

Again, then, the appearance of complementarity: which makes it more striking that in fact her joy and Nemours's are subtly different. Her joy is pure pleasure in the sight of Nemours: earlier (263), her love was attributed to her perception of his superiority to all other men: yet where that love and that joy tend, or whether perhaps they are ends in themselves, is unclear. In his case, it is not clear, as will be seen if we revert to the occasions of joy mentioned above. On the first, his enjoyment is in having the portrait of Mme de Clèves, and in what the incident portends:

> Il aimait la plus aimable personne de la Cour; il s'en faisait aimer malgré elle,
> et il voyait dans toutes ses actions cette sorte de trouble et d'embarras que
> cause l'amour dans innocence de la première jeunesse. (303)

On the second, he is pleased by the bitterness of her tone (324), having already decided that coldness was an encouraging sign, inasmuch as it might well betoken jealousy (323). On the third, his pleasure is in having reduced her to the extremity of the confession (337). After seeing her in the *pavillon*, he rejoices at finding her 'si remplie de son idée' (368). Naomi Schor's analysis is acute and pertinent: 'What he beholds is his own likeness as viewed through the eyes of an adoring woman. *Jouissance* for Nemours is being the spectator of his own desirability.'[28]

The final occasion of joy is the Princess's avowal, and this rounds off the point: what Nemours desires, to return to Blake again, is the lineaments of his own gratified desire. His joy is in the foretaste each sign gives him of the ultimate joy of her avowing her subjection, in the sense of her recognition that she is possessed by the idea of him. So much is this so that he even entertains the idea that this is all he wants:

Laissez-moi voir que vous m'aimez, belle princesse, s'écria-t-il, laissez-moi voir
vos sentiments; pourvu que je les connaisse *par vous* une fois en ma vie, je
consens que vous repreniez pour toujours ces rigueurs dont vous m'accabliez.
(369: my italics)

The text does not conceal the element of violence in this: 'il s'en faisait
aimer malgré elle', 'l'avoir reduitte à cette extrémité'.[29] At one point, indeed, he
expresses (to himself) his grief at the pain he has caused her, more intense than
the disappointment he feels at having spoiled his chances of having her (353).

The tonality of M. de Clèves's feelings is quite different: so much so that
Claudine Herrmann perceives him as 'un homme féminisé, ou plutôt un de ces
rares individus qui possèdent en eux les deux mondes [...] le rêve de Mme de
Lafayette'; a Utopian figure, who escapes the competition for superiority,
content to be simply different.[30] Even so, he partakes in some ways of the same
masculine universe as Nemours. Joy, of course, is rare for him (unlike Nemours
he has no reason to believe himself loved); but like Nemours he makes it plain
that his desire is for her desire:

Il la pressa de lui faire connoître quels étaient les sentiments qu'elle avait pour
lui et il lui dit que ceux qu'il avait pour elle étaient d'une nature qui le rend-
rait éternellement malheureux si elle n'obéissait que par devoir aux volontés
de madame sa mère. (257)

He does once, however, express his happiness in striking terms:

Les femmes sont incompréhensibles et, quand je les vois toutes, je me trouve
si heureux de vous avoir que je ne saurois assez admirer mon bonheur. (280)

He does not say exactly what he believes makes her different from other
women, but since the context is the story of Mme de Tournon's duplicity, and
other women are incomprehensible, it must be that her virtue is authentic and
transparent. This takes us back to the whole problem of the motivation of
passion. When the Princess first appears to M. de Clèves, what strikes him, as
we saw, was her beauty and her modesty. With Nemours (262) it is her beauty

that makes the impact. Later, however, it becomes clear that what the Duke desires in her is connected with her modesty: he desires her because he knows she is in love with him in spite of herself, so that he owes his triumph entirely to his own attractions (not to any spontaneous desire of hers).

This certainly disturbs the image of complementarity, for it shows that there is, in Naomi Schor's words:

> a notable difference between male and female difference: to be unique among her sex a woman must practise an exemplary virtue [...] whereas to rise above his peers a man must refrain from advertising his conquests.[31]

The woman's virtue is requisite to the masculine system of values not only as a guarantee of fidelity but as proof that the desire directed at oneself is one's own creation, and not due to any female libidinousness that might have been satisfied by some other male.

Yet the Duke's desire is associated not just with the heroine's virtue, in the narrow sense of chastity, but with an even more individual quality. For when we are told that 'il trouva de la gloire à s'être fait aimer d'une femme si différente de toutes celles de son sexe'(337), it is in the aftermath of her confession. So her difference lies partly in a quality, her sincerity, the uniqueness of which was first asserted in connexion with not a man's but a woman's reaction to her: 'Mme de Chartres admirait la sincérité de sa fille, et elle l'admirait avec raison, car jamais personne n'en a eu une si grande et si naturelle' (259). Here is a unique excellence that does not feature within the scheme of values of courtly perfection in conformity to which the Princess and Nemours initially love each other. It enhances Nemours's passion, his sense of glory, as we have seen. Yet at the same time it imparts a certain perversity to his attachment; as if, in loving the Princess, he finds he is not exactly loving a woman. (As Claudine Herrmann subtly observes 'la princesse de Clèves éveille l'admiration beaucoup plus parce qu'elle est "honnête homme" que parce qu'elle est "honnête femme"').[32] She herself alludes to her sincerity, and to him, as an unfeminine characteristic:

> Puisque vous voulez que je vous parle et que je m'y résous [...] je le ferai avec
> une sincérité que vous trouverez malaisément dans les personnes de mon sexe.
> (383)

The sincerity, lifting the Princess out of the world of courtly excellence, in a
sense constitutes her as an object that subsumes courtly values within an order
unthinkable within the limits of the courtly imagination. She has 'tout ce qui
peut faire une adorable maîtresse' (386); but mistresses at court are always objects of competition, and even Nemours can fear a rival. Marriage makes no
difference, for we have seen that the marriage bond is not respected; and indeed
marriage in a sense accentuates the basic fear of other men that subtends male
desire in the book, by conjuring up the risk of shame as well as grief at infidelity:

> Tous ceux qui épousent des maîtresses dont ils sont aimés, tremblent en les
> épousant, et regardent avec crainte, par rapport aux autres, la conduite qu'elles
> ont eue avec eux. (383)

The Princess's difference banishes such fears, for she has 'tout ce qui peut être à
désirer dans une femme': 'en vous, madame, rien n'est à craindre, et on ne
trouve que des sujets d'admiration' (383). Here then is what Nemours sees as
her true uniqueness, which fits her to be the ultimate object of desire for a man:
her capacity for love, which befits a mistress, reflects him in the most flattering
terms, her wifely qualities assure him that he need not fear for the future of this
relationship: 'vous estes peut-être la seule personne en qui ces deux choses se
soient jamais trouvées au degré qu'elles sont en vous' (386). Delight without
fear. 'Il dépend de vous de faire en sorte que votre devoir vous oblige un jour à
conserver les sentiments que vous avez pour moi.' (385)

 What makes the Princess the perfect wife, in Nemours's eyes, is thus her
high regard for duty. There is of course the problem that that sense of duty
leads her to think that she is not, morally speaking, free to marry Nemours, in
that he is as much responsible for her husband's death as if he had killed him in
a duel (the 'extrémités' to which she refers (385)).[33] But there is also the prob-

lem that her uniqueness, which makes her so desirable, partly consists in her sincerity: that is, her capacity to put her feelings into discourse, and thus distance herself from them.[34] Her confession is not just an expression of her feelings, but, as Joan DeJean has well suggested, it partakes of the old sense of *aveu*: an oath of loyalty.[35] It has a performative value, which lends force to her declaration that 'si j'ai des sentiments qui vous déplaisent, du moins je ne vous déplairai jamais par mes actions' (333–34). Likewise, in her conversation with Nemours, she is not simply releasing the information that she loves him, so that he could conclude that, inevitably, she must yield to him. She is performing another kind of *aveu*: when she says 'Je vous avoue donc, non seulement que l'ai vu [*sc.* l'attachement que vous avez eu pour moi], mais que je l'ai vu tel que vous pouvez souhaiter qu'il m'ait paru' (383), she is recognizing his devotion, validating his own sense of the integrity and intensity of his love; and later, when she says 'je vous avoue que vous m'avez inspiré des sentiments qui m'étaient inconnus devant que de vous avoir vu' (189), she is, so to speak, formally certifying her feelings for him, and thus unwittingly fulfilling the wish he expressed among the willows near Coulommiers, that she would herself declare her feelings to him. But it is as if she has heard not only the wish, but the conditions he was prepared to attach to its fulfilment: 'je consens que vous repreniez pour toujours ces rigueurs dont vous m'accabliez' (369). Her sincerity is more than the capacity to make true statements about her feelings: it is the quality that underlies her making of *declarations* by which she intends to be bound. It can thus conduce to a behaviour-pattern that negates her feelings, no less than to acting in conformity with them. As such, it is almost, from Nemours's viewpoint, a superfluous virtue: analogous to 'the one thing, to my purpose nothing' of which Shakespeare speaks in Sonnet I; and Nemours emerges as a kind of proto-Sarrasine trapped in a fatal desire for an object that exceeds and transgresses gender categories (in this case, by assuming the status of subject). Perhaps, after all, she (sincerity and all) is not 'what men want'.

The Princess indeed stands Freud's notorious question, 'What do women want?', on its head. 'Son education lui permet d'entrevoir ceci: les hommes et les femmes échangent des sentiments qui ne sont pas equivalents', suggests Claudine Herrmann:[36] if this were so it would be because their desires are incommensurable, incapable of harmonisation. As we know, the heroine's refusal is largely prompted by her doubt as to how far Nemours himself can be excepted from the masculine norm: 'Les hommes conservent-ils de la passion dans ces engagements éternels?' (387), and as to whether individual character can be definitively suspended by passion: 'Vous êtes né avec toutes les dispositions pour la galanterie et toutes les qualités qui sont propres à y donner des succès heureux' (387). What does Nemours want: lasting passion in marriage (he speaks of 'l'espérance de passer ma vie avec vous' (386)), or a woman who will not only reciprocate his passion, but who, if or when it fades on his side, will none the less remain faithful to him? Men's constancy, in the Princess's experience, whether that of her husband or that of Nemours up to this point, is always linked to frustration, and she would have no means of conserving Nemours's feelings in this way (387).[37]

Such means exist, however. They are those put into effect by the Duchesse de Valentinois, who, as is often pointed out, retains the King's affection to his death.[38] In other words what men (some men? sometimes?) seem to want may not conform at all to the economy in which women's desirability is enhanced by their resistance. What the Duchess has or does is not totally clear: it seems to be a combination both of endowing Henri with his masculinity (the 'hardiesse' and the 'vivacité' that his father complained he lacked (266)) and of constantly challenging it by her infidelities. But the text is sufficiently discreet for it to be unclear to us what answer it proposes to the question of what men want.

Yet whether in any case all this matters to the Princess is another enigma that the text does not resolve. For to wish to keep the affections of a particular man by the application of particular seductive arts, it is necessary to believe that, for some purpose, this man differs from others: in other words, to participate in the courtly *illusio*. It is easy to think that the Princess's decision turns on her inability to decide whether Nemours is different (from other men or from his previous self). Certainly, her last communication with him specifically says that, since her inclination to give herself to him has been overcome by considerations of *devoir* and *repos*, 'les autres choses du monde lui avaient paru si indifférentes qu'elle y avait renoncé pour jamais' (394). This preserves

Nemours's difference, but the end-result of the decision is to define her previous dilemma as in-different (it does not matter what Nemours is since she is not going to be with him): to break entirely with the courtly, that is, the amorous, *illusio*.

QUEEN MARY AND WESTFIELD COLLEGE, LONDON

NOTES

1. Aristotle, *Nicomachean Ethics*, ed. and trans. by H. Rackham, Loeb Classical Library (London: Heinemann, and Cambridge, MA: Harvard University Press, 1947), VI.5.1 (1140a).

2. John Campbell, *Questions of Interpretation in 'La Princesse de Clèves'*, Faux Titre, 108 (Amsterdam: Rodopi, 1986), p. 204: see also pp. 14–55, and in particular pp. 23–31. Campbell's argument rules out the view that the Princess is actuated by irrational feelings; but it does not preclude psychoanalytic or other explanations that postulate unconscious causation, since actions, whatever the reasons behind them, may always signify more than the agent is aware of.

3. Aristotle, *Rhetoric*, I.ii.15 (1357a), in Aristotle, *The 'Art' of Rhetoric*, ed. and trans. by John Henry Freese, Loeb Classical Library (Cambridge, MA: Harvard University Press, 1982). 'Can be other than they are' in this translation is an exact equivalent of 'admit of variation' in the other, the corresponding Greek expression being *allôs echein*. The point is to distinguish the realm of prudence, in the one case, and rhetorical discourse, in the other, from that of scientific knowledge (*epistêmê*), which deals with that which does not 'admit of variation' or 'cannot be other than it is'. This authorises us to equate, for this purpose, the domain of prudential deliberation with that of rhetoric.

4. See Gerard Genette, 'Vraisemblance et motivation', in *Figures II* (Paris: Seuil, 1969), pp. 71–99; Nancy K. Miller, 'Emphasis Added: Plots and Plausibilities in Women's Fiction', *Proceedings of the Modern Language Society of America*, 96 (1981), 36–48: reprinted in *An Inimitable Example: the Case for the Princesse de Clèves*, ed. by Patrick Henry (Washington, DC: Catholic University of America Press, 1992), pp. 15–38; Steven Rendall, 'Trapped between Romance and Novel: a Defense of the Princesse de Clèves', in *An Inimitable Example*, pp. 127–38.

5. Jules Brody, relating the text to the courtly love tradition, puts the question as follows: 'Has the heroine found in Nemours one of those rare and beautiful souls

capable of restoring to the time-worn courtly myth some of its lost spiritual substance?' ('*La Princesse de Clèves* and the Myth of Courtly Love', *University of Toronto Quarterly*, 38 (1969), 105–35 (p. 110)).

6. See, e.g. Brody, p. 106.

7. Susan W. Tiefenbrun, *A Structural Stylistic Analysis of 'La Princesse de Clèves'* (The Hague: Mouton, 1976), p. 27. See also Peter Bayley, 'Fixed Form and Varied Function: Reflexions on the Language of French Classicism', *Seventeenth-Century French Studies*, 6 (1984), 6–21.

8. Ralph Albanese, Jr., 'Aristocratic Ethos and Ideological Codes in *La Princesse de Clèves*', in *An Inimitable Example*, pp. 87-103 (pp. 10–12); and cp. Philippe Desan, 'The Economy of Love in *La Princesse de Clèves*', in *An Inimitable Example*, pp. 104–24 (p. 123).

9.

> Loretta was disgusted. They were arguing about cricket. One of their colleagues had vanished in mysterious circumstances and all they could do was make up imaginary England cricket teams.

Joan Smith, *A Masculine Ending* (London: Faber & Faber, 1987), pp. 59–60.

10. Smith, *A Masculine Ending*, p. 59.

11. On 'field' and 'habitus', see, for instance, Pierre Bourdieu and Loïc J. D. Wacquant, *Réponses: Pour une anthropologie réflexive* (Paris: Seuil, 1992), pp. 24, 72–73.

12. Bourdieu, *Les Règles de l'art: Genèse et structure du champ littéraire* (Paris: Seuil, 1992), p. 316.

13. Madame de Lafayette, *La Princesse de Clèves*, in *Romans et nouvelles*, ed. by Émile Magne and Alain Niderst, Classiques Garnier (Paris: Garnier, 1970), pp. 237–395 (p. 319). All future references will be to this edition and will be given in parentheses in the text.

14. Marivaux, *La Double Inconstance*, III.8.

15. See Campbell's excellent analysis (pp. 74–79).

16. On different understandings of love in this sentence, see Marianne Hirsch, 'A Mother's Discourse: Incorporation and Repetition in *La Princesse de Clèves*', *Yale French Studies*, 62 (1981), 67–87 (p. 75).

17. Jean-Baptiste-Henri du Trousset de Valincour, *Lettres à Madame la Marquise *** sur le sujet de 'La Princesse de Clèves'*, ed. by Albert Cazes, Les Chefs d'Œuvre Méconnus (Paris: Bossard, 1925), pp. 95, 155.

18. On complementarity, see Helen Karen Kaps, *Moral Perspective in 'La Princesse de Clèves'* (Eugene: University of Oregon Books, 1968), p. 40, and Brody, p. 106 (Brody goes on to question the extent of this complementarity, as do various other critics:

see below). A persuasive reading of this complementarity as imaginary in a (richly exploited) psychoanalytical sense is put forward by Mitchell Greenberg, *Subjectivity and Subjugation in Seventeenth-Century French Drama and Prose: the Family Romance of French Classicism*, Cambridge Studies in French, 36 (Cambridge: Cambridge University Press, 1992), pp. 197–98.

19. Philippe Desan seeks to analyse the workings of the court as a market. Whether or not one accepts the whole of his argument, the following remark is suggestive: women are 'a medium of exchange that allows men to accrue value by participating in economic transactions' ('The Economy of Love in *La Princesse de Clèves*', in *An Inimitable Example*, pp. 104–24 (pp. 105–06)).

20. On the relationship between male participants and female onlookers, see Michael Danahy, *The Feminization of the Novel*, University of Florida Humanities Monographs, 65 (Gainesville: University of Florida Press, 1991), pp. 107–08.

21. On his entry see Barbara Woshinsky, '*La Princesse de Clèves*': the Tension of Elegance*, De Proprietatibus Litterarum, Series Practica, 72 (The Hague: Mouton, 1973), p. 76; and also Danahy, p. 104.

22. Jean-Michel Delacomptée, '*La Princesse de Clèves*': La Mère et le courtisan* (Paris: Presses Universitaires de France, 1990), p. 109. He goes on to remark that 'l'amitié n'est qu'une rivalité primaire épurée de sa haine'(ibid.).

23. In *La Comtesse de Tende*, the heroine feels she has betrayed her friend the Princesse de Neufchâtel by accepting the love of the Chevalier de Navarre (Mme de Lafayette, *La Comtesse de Tende*, in *Romans et nouvelles*, pp. 397–412 (p. 400)).

24. Albanese, p. 101.

25. Not that Christian morality is irrelevant to the text as a whole: several critics have demonstrated the Christian resonances of the ending (even though, so to speak, the coif does not make the nun). The point is simply that Christian morality does not seem to affect most of the decisions taken by the bulk of the characters.

26. The point is urged by Michael S. Koppisch, 'The Princesse de Clèves's Will to Order', in *An Inimitable Example*, pp. 195–208 (p. 206).

27.

> Lorsqu'on analyse un texte, à tout instant, nous devons réagir contre l'impression d'évidence, le 'cela-va-de-soi' de ce qui est écrit. [...] Il faut toujours penser à ce qui se passerait si le trait n'était pas noté ou s'il était différent.

'L'Analyse structurale du récit: à propos d'*Actes*, 10–11' in Roland Barthes, *Œuvres complètes*, ed. by Éric Marty, 3 vols (Paris: Seuil, 1993–95 (II, 846)).

28. Naomi Schor, 'The Portrait of a Gentleman: Representing Men in (French) Women's Writing', in *Bad Objects: Essays Popular and Unpopular* (Duke University Press: Durham and London, 1995, pp. 111–31 (p. 117) (previously in *Representations*, 20 (Fall 1987), 113–33).

29. On the aggressiveness of passion, see Campbell, pp. 32–33.

30. Claudine Herrmann, *Les Voleuses de langue* (Paris: Des Femmes, 1976) p. 46.

31. Schor, p. 119. It was the Princess herself who thought, as she realises, erroneously, that what made Nemours different from other men was his discretion (352).

32. Herrmann, p. 25.

33. On the heroine's interpretation of her duty, see Kaps, pp. 20–21, and Rendall, pp. 127–35.

34. On the Princess's self-distancing from direct experience, see Campbell, p. 157: he wisely cautions that this is not to be automatically equated with lucidity.

35. Joan DeJean, 'Lafayette's Ellipses: the Privileges of Anonymity', in *An Inimitable Example*, pp. 39–70 (p. 64) (originally in *PMLA*, 99 (1984), 884–902).

36. Herrmann, p. 78

37. J.-M. Delacomptée argues that the men in the novel do not conform to the model alluded to by the heroine in which women are desirable only as objects to be conquered, then discarded: 'C'est le sentiment rendu et reconnu qui soutient ce choix, pas la résistance' (p. 16). Men certainly desire the recognition of their desire. Yet there is enough fairly casual infidelity on men's part to suggest the general plausibility of the model.

38. Anne Green observes that the strategy of Mme de Valentinois has been prefigured by the Marquise de Noirmoutier in *La Princesse de Montpensier*, who is similarly both more forthcoming with her lovers and more blatantly unfaithful to them (*Privileged Anonymity: the Writings of Madame de Lafayette*, Research Monographs in French Studies, 1 (Oxford: European Humanities Research Centre, 1996), p. 72; and cf. p. 49 and Madame de Lafayette, *Romans et nouvelles*, pp. 32–33). John D. Lyons stresses the subversive effect of Mme de Valentinois's behaviour on Mme de Chartres's empirical discourse of the passions ('Narrative, Interpretation and Paradox: *La Princesse de Clèves*', *Romanic Review*, 72 (1981), 383–400 (p. 393)).

SHIRLEY JONES DAY

Madame d'Aulnoy's Julie: a heroine of the 1690s

Nancy Miller's definition of the heroine's text in the eighteenth-century novel as one where she is presented in the context of a clearly defined moral code,[1] is particularly appropriate to a tradition of fiction which has its roots in the late seventeenth century and whose importance has, up to now, escaped critical attention. I refer to the writings of women novelists who, more than their male counterparts who are familiar to us, foreshadow the novel of the eighteenth century in its commonly held insistence on the correlation between desire and socially accepted morality.

This definition can of course be construed as one of the main themes of the literary masterpiece of an earlier generation, *La Princesse de Clèves*. However, as recent criticism has rightly shown, Mme de Lafayette's work, because of its subtlety, defied definition for its contemporaries as it still does for us.[2] What is important as far as women contemporaries are concerned is what they thought they saw in *La Princesse de Clèves*: in practical terms, what women writers following in Mme de Lafayette's footsteps chose to imitate in their own fictions. During the last decade of the seventeenth century, three women writers in particular, Mlle Bernard,[3] Mme d'Aulnoy,[4] and Mlle de La Force,[5] took up the theme of the heroine as unmarried girl and then as wife, which they developed with significant modifications. All three were clearly inspired by Mme de Lafayette's text. There is equally clear evidence of mutual influences within these feminocentric texts which take as their subject matter the clash between passion and society. Although all three of these women novelists enjoyed a considerable success, which lasted well beyond their lifetime, all have long since been forgotten; and whilst Mlle Bernard has of recent years received serious critical attention,[6] the historical fiction of the most innovative (and the most successful) of the three novelists, Mme d'Aulnoy, has not yet been rescued from the oblivion into which it has fallen. While she is acknowledged as an author of *contes de fées*,[7] she has been excluded from the literary pantheon properly speaking,[8] so that her fate seems aptly to illustrate Joan DeJean's thesis that women's writing of the Classical period and beyond, which initially enjoyed a considerable popularity, was, during the course of the eighteenth century expunged from the literary canon.[9]

Mme d'Aulnoy's first novel, the *Histoire d'Hypolite, comte de Duglas*, published in 1690, was a best seller.[10] The story, which is set in England at the time of the Reformation, centres on the love of the heroine, Julie, for Hypolite, the son of a Scottish nobleman, Milord de Duglas. In telling her heroine's tale, Mme d'Aulnoy deals with the important phases of a woman's life: early childhood; adolescence and emotional awakening; a first unhappy marriage, which brings with it no emotional fulfilment, before the final scene of the happy ending when Julie and Hypolite are at last united in marriage.

The first phase of the story begins with Julie's being effectively orphaned. Her father, the comte de Warwick, is forced to flee the country to escape political persecution. News reaches his wife that he has been killed fighting the pirate Dragut Rais and she dies soon after of a broken heart, leaving the infant Julie in the care of fellow recusants, Milord and Madame de Duglas, who have two children, Hypolite and Lucile, and who bring Julie up as their own daughter. Adolescence brings with it suffering in that Julie and Hypolite fall in love and are racked with guilt, believing that their passion is incestuous. Taking the onus of guilt on herself, Julie decides to leave the world and become a nun; and it is this decision that sets the action in motion through the dual revelations that it provokes. First, Julie's 'parents' reveal to her the secret of her birth, a knowledge that sets the lovers free from their (false) sense of guilt. For them, their love is innocent and therefore good. Second, the lovers' secret, that of their mutual passion, is discovered by Hypolite's parents, who, in the name of family, that is to say, material interests, oppose their love.

The battle lines are thus drawn up. On the one hand, the parent figures invested with power, moved solely by material considerations, whilst the lovers are presented as outsiders: Julie, the orphan figure, and Hypolite, the son who is entirely in his father's power. The conflict that ensues between passion and social values leads to an alienation between the lovers and society which is eventually expressed in terms of physical exile. Hypolite is packed off to Italy (encountering en route Julie's father, who had simply been taken captive by Dragut Rais). Attempts are made to alienate the lovers from each other; and eventually Julie is tricked into marriage with a man she cannot love, the comte de Bedfort.

Julie's marriage to Bedfort is presented as a worse form of tyranny than that which she had suffered at the hands of her 'family'. Victim of her husband's jealous passion, she feels that even her thoughts are no longer her own. She is a virtual prisoner in her husband's home; and following an attempt on Hypolite's part to see her, she is secretly borne off by Bedfort to be held prisoner in a convent in France. Finally, a series of more or less implausible adventures serves to reunite the lovers with Julie's father and to kill off the odious husband, Bedfort, so that Julie's and Hypolite's story ends with their reintegration into society as man and wife.

Taken as the heroine's text, one that deals specifically with feminine destiny, analogies between Julie's story and that of Mme de Lafayette's heroine, Mlle de Chartres, necessarily present themselves. However, the fundamental shift in moral attitude on the part of the woman writer in this 1690s text from that of the 1670s is implicit from the outset in the account of her heroine and her world; and apparent similarities of plot, in the sense that both stories trace the heroine's progression from girlhood to marriage, serve to point up these fundamental differences.

Taking the role of childhood experiences in both stories: Mlle de Chartres, like Julie, is brought up far from court, in a sheltered environment. In Mme de Lafayette's text, the intense mother/daughter relationship constitutes one of the key elements that shape the course of the story, a relationship based on a transparency that is shattered, not by the heroine's marriage, but by the awakening of her desire for Nemours. Moreover, a significant feature of the mother/daughter nexus in *La Princesse de Clèves* is that it is placed in the context of a gynaecocratic environment — Mme de Chartres is an empowered widow. Mlle de Chartres's destiny is inscribed in this initial situation: she *knows* who she is, 'une des plus grandes héritières de France'.[11] Her moral and emotional identity has been initially shaped by her mother's teaching. The problem that later confronts her when she falls in love with a man other than her husband must, in the light of these initial givens, be formulated in terms of an interiorized moral code.

The picture of Julie's background and early experience stands in stark contrast to that of Mlle de Chartres. In place of the loving mother we are confronted with a patriarchal society where parent figures, who are false in more than one sense, represent an authority which punishes rather than protects; and whose attitude to their foster daughter is summed up by Milord de Duglas's statement that: 'encore qu'elle ne soit pas notre fille, elle dépend assez de nous pour pouvoir faire le bonheur ou le malheur de sa vie' (52). It is precisely Julie's status as an outsider that informs the moral structure of the work. Whereas *La Princesse de Clèves* is fundamentally a novel of education and therefore, in an important sense, a novel of sociability, in Mme d'Aulnoy's text, the question of sociability is not posed.

Most important, the transparency which characterized Mlle de Chartres's relationship with her mother is replaced in Julie's case by a situation which is essentially based on a deception of which she remains the victim. In the beginning a deceit was practised on her for reasons of political or religious expediency, for which society at large was to blame. The injustice is then seen to be perpetuated by the family, representing social values based on financial or dynastic considerations. The truth about Julie's birth is revealed to be worthless in social terms, since it does not bring with it money or powerful relatives. As a penniless nobody she is an unfitting wife for Hypolite. Society, as represented by the family, is shown to be the enemy of individual freedom.

In her relations with society, the revelation of the truth of her identity serves merely to deprive Julie of her (false) identity without endowing her with a socially valid one: she remains simply Julie, in effect an orphan. It is this factor that most clearly defines the contrast between her situation and that of Mlle de Chartres: Julie is referred to simply by her first name, an indication of her socially ambiguous status. She is moreover the first of a long line of English heroines in French literature. However, Mme d'Aulnoy's seminal importance in women's writing lies in the fact that, through Julie, she explores the problems confronting the unmarried girl in a materialistic society.[12] Manifestly, the social tone in Mme d'Aulnoy's text has descended a notch from that of *La Princesse de Clèves*; and through her portrayal of her heroine, Julie, money has entered the novel as a theme of primary importance, specifically as it related to women's experience, in terms of the dowry without which their passage into the adult life was restricted.[13]

It is in her portrayal of Julie as an unmarried girl at odds with social conventions that the originality of Mme d'Aulnoy's literary creation is most striking. Simply as Julie, the supposed daughter of Milord de Duglas, her individuality is sharply delineated. Her creator has endowed her with a certain capacity for dissembling in her relations with her foster parents, and for attempting to manipulate a fundamentally unfavourable situation in her favour. When she is condemned by Milord and Madame de Duglas for daring to consider herself worthy of becoming Hypolite's wife, she retorts: 'J'ay entendu dire que l'union des cœurs est indispensablement necessaire dans un établissement qui ne doit finir qu'avec la vie' (33).

Taking these two phrases, 'l'union des cœurs', and 'un établissement qui ne doit finir qu'avec la vie', I want to define Julie, and through her the image of female destiny presented by a woman writer of the 1690s. The reference to 'un établissement qui ne doit finir qu'avec la vie' calls to mind the great scene at the end of the story of Mme de Clèves and Nemours, when she rejects the possibility of marriage to him on the grounds that marriage, which represents sociability in its most institutionalised form, is in the long run incompatible with passion.[14] In *La Princesse de Clèves*, the heroine's moral standpoint is that of an insider: Mme de Clèves never questions, let alone challenges, the moral laws governing the conduct of the *'honnête femme'*.[15] For Julie however, the decision to reject social laws in the name of passion is taken at the outset of her story. The ideal she proposes, *l'union des cœurs*, directly challenges the view of marriage as a socio-economic arrangement. In the view of marriage she propounds, individual happiness is assured, and consequently the nature of passion is never questioned.

If Mme d'Aulnoy's portrait of family relationships is a bleak one, her portrait of marriage is bleaker still. On her wedding day, Julie appears at the altar like a sacrificial victim. We are given a meticulous description of Julie's dress:

un habit de brocard d'argent blanc, chamaré d'une dentelle mêlée de couleur
de rose & d'argent, elle avoit beaucoup de Pierreries, ses cheveux blonds
estoient ornez de fleurs. (75)

In this the only description of dress in the book, the narrator views her heroine
from the point of view of the onlooker. Its effect is to emphasize the contrast
between the material appearance of wealth, symbolic of social values, and the
inner reality of individual unhappiness.

That marriage constitutes an even greater denial of a woman's liberty
than the single state is made clear in the text in the recurrent theme of imprisonment that is a leitmotif of the second part of the novel. On her marriage to
Bedfort, Julie is carried off and kept out of sight in her husband's magnificent
country mansion which is surrounded by forests. She is then carried off and
imprisoned once more when Bedfort discovers that she and Hypolite are in
love.

Equally significant is the change in the heroine's character following her
marriage. From the fearless and resourceful girl of the first part, she becomes
cowed and passive. Immediately after her marriage, she confides her dilemma to
Hypolite's sister, Lucile, that even her thoughts are no longer her own.[16] She is
kept locked away, guarded by a jealous husband — Bedfort is invariably described as *jaloux* or referred to as *son jaloux*. This change in personality is de
noted by a change in the language she uses. In place of bold claims for *l'union
des cœurs*, we now have constant references to a moral code expressed in language coined by an earlier generation: terms like *ma gloire*, which had long
since lost their moral force, and which by their archaic nature indicate that Julie
has dwindled into a wife, a mere puppet mouthing moral platitudes.

Her total passivity is complementary to the theme of the total and arbitrary power of her husband, who, with the approval of society, can carry her
off and imprison her at will. The themes of women's lack of status within
marriage and of conjugal violence, which Julie's story illustrates, given their
relevance to the reality of marriage in the late seventeenth century, were bound
to appeal to the woman writer and reader. Mme d'Aulnoy's subject matter: the
harsh reality of the institution of marriage that gave the husband unlimited

power over his wife (and particularly a wife who brought no dowry into the marriage, as was Julie's case) was part of the experience of seventeenth-century women. Violence against women within marriage was, as Olwen Hufton has shown in her recent study, both common and socially acceptable.[17] However, these topics were difficult to render in terms of the literary conventions of the time; and the problems which such subject matter posed for the late seventeenth-century woman novelist arguably constitute an important factor influencing the narrative structure in the second part of Mme d'Aulnoy's novel. In real life, Julie would have remained at the mercy of her bullying husband, so that it was only by having recourse to the world of fantasy and romance that Mme d'Aulnoy could contrive a happy ending. One could moreover argue that a non-realistic treatment of the theme of conjugal violence was imposed on a woman writer by a society that refused to acknowledge the existence of this violence.

The full significance of Mme d'Aulnoy's creation of her heroine, from the point of view both of the aesthetics of her novel and of its underlying moral message, merits a detailed examination which would go beyond the scope of the present discussion. There can be no doubt, however, that in Julie we have an image of woman that was new in the novel and was destined to have a consider-able influence on later writers: the image of woman as victim of society, more-over, a victim who represents values which are at variance with those of a materialistic society. Mme d'Aulnoy's championing, through Julie, of the hero-ine's right to follow the dictates of her own heart constitutes both an important rehabilitation of the passions and, as its corollary, an indictment of a society where marriage was a matter of socio-economic convenience. The character of Julie is the cornerstone of the work; and each of the other characters must be read in the context of what she represents. Mme d'Aulnoy's criticism of the institutions of the family and marriage are mediated through Julie's experience, and the radical nature of this criticism is most clearly understood when com-pared with *La Princesse de Clèves* (also a novel dealing with family relationships and marriage). The coherent aesthetic pattern which underlies the work is first discernible in Mme d'Aulnoy's use of the historical framework as a distancing device, in contrast with *La Princesse de Clèves*, where a precise historical setting frames a novel of sociability. In the *Histoire d'Hypolite*, the macro-context of history which functions at one remove from the plot itself (the account of the political events which precede the opening of the action), the material background of mansions surrounded by forests, all combine to create the image of the heroine as an isolated figure. And it is this image of isolation that defines the heroine within the micro-context of the family: the dead or absent parents, the unloving surrogate parents, the mystery that hangs over her true identity, each of these gives the clue to the strategy employed here, that of the *conte de fées*. Julie the orphan, deprived of her status within the family power structure is in fact a Cinderella figure; and in her creation of the 'false' parents and the nightmarish husband, Mme d'Aulnoy has made subtle use of the conventions of the fairy story to create a parable of late seventeenth-century woman's experience. Mme d'Aulnoy the author of brilliant *contes de fées* is, in many senses of the term, one and the same person as the author of now-forgotten historical novels.[18]

This perhaps leaves us with the question of why she chose to give this quintessentially feminocentric text, not the name of her heroine, whose character clearly informs the work's structure and aesthetics, but that of her hero, Hypolite. Leaving aside speculation about the writer's intentions which cannot be substantiated by documentary evidence, I would argue that the answer lies in some measure in the text itself. If the comte de Bedfort represents the antithesis of the tragic and dignified figure of Clèves as the husband, then Hypolite represents an equally diametrically opposite model of the lover from Nemours. Where Nemours's sexual experience is an important feature of Mme de Lafayette's story,[19] Hypolite is portrayed as the innocent youth. As he touchingly confides to his Italian friend, Leandre, 'J'aimois Julie avant que de me connoistre moy-même' (69). This portrait of the hero as being the male counterpart of the heroine is further enhanced by the sensibility with which he is endowed. It is he, even more than Julie, who is represented in the grip of powerful emotions, weeping, fainting, lying prostrate, subject to psychosomatic illness. Let us look, for instance, at Hypolite's reaction to Julie's decision to enter a convent and consequently to be parted from him for ever:

[Julie] trouva Hypolite couché sur un lit de repos, le visage couvert de son mouchoir; lorsqu'elle parut il voulut se lever, mais ses forces lui manquant, il retomba sur le même lit. Julie s'approcha de lui, & prenant sa main qu'elle serra entre les siennes, elle le regarda quelque temps les yeux pleins de larmes. Mon frere, lui dit-elle, aprés un assez long silence, l'état où je vous vois me penetre de douleur. (21)

This short extract from an important episode in the story encapsulates the respective characters of the hero and heroine, he, totally in the grip of his emotions whereas as she plays a more decisive role. He is weak and helpless, she is strong and courageous.

Could it not be seen that in creating Hypolite, Mme d'Aulnoy has colonized, has 'feminized' so to speak, the space reserved for the hero as representing traditionally 'masculine' values, so that in Hypolite too we have an extension of the heroine's text? The closure of the novel leads me towards such an interpretation: ' Hypolite prit le titre de Comte de Duglas, sous lequel il s'est fait connoître pour un des plus polis, & des plus braves hommes de son siecle' (173). Thus, after several hundred pages devoted to Hypolite as lover of Julie, his public exploits are dealt with in a few lines. So much for the masculine values that, as Joan DeJean has pointed out, eighteenth-century critics came to view as the touchstone of literary worth; and little wonder that critics like the Abbé Batteux should have decided that such a Heroine's Text as Julie's story should be consigned to oblivion.[20]

The reference in my title to the period when Mme d'Aulnoy created her heroine, the 1690s, clearly must place it in relation to the masterpiece of women's writing of the 1670s, *La Princesse de Clèves*. With similar logic, the question of the relationship between the heroine of the 1690s and those of the 1730s — or even the 1760s — should be addressed if one is to attempt a comprehensive definition of Julie's place in literary history. Put simply, how isolated a figure in literary history is Mme d'Aulnoy's Julie? The oblivion which has engulfed women's fiction from the 1670s onwards both tempts one to examine its causes and makes it difficult to decide how total is the eclipse of the woman writer after Mme de Lafayette. Is it true that, from having been a powerful figure in prose fiction from the mid century to the late 70s, inspiration suddenly deserted the woman writer?

Given our current lack of knowledge where women's writing post-Lafayette is concerned, to attempt to identify Mme d'Aulnoy's Julie's literary progeny would be a vast — and highly contentious — enterprise.[21] However, the very name Mme d'Aulnoy chose for her heroine, Julie, prompts at least some initial musings on the subject of two fictional heroines of the eighteenth century: the narrator's sister in Prévost's first major work of fiction, the *Mémoires et aventures d'un homme de qualité*, and, of course, the century's most famous fictional heroine, Rousseau's Julie.

The *Mémoires et aventures d'un homme de qualité* is a seminal work in the canon of Prévost's fiction.[22] In it he makes extensive use of the literary *topoi* that formed part of an essentially feminine literary tradition: plots that defy the classical code of verisimilitude in that they rely on such devices as chance encounters and journeys to distant lands.[23] In addition to these structural devices, the pivotal theme of the *Mémoires d'un homme de qualité*: the conflict between passion and society, echoes the thematic structure of the Aulnoy model, as does the psychology of the principal male characters: Renoncour the narrator; his young ward Rosemont; and, in the famous seventh book of the novel, Des Grieux himself. All are *jeunes téméraires*. Each of the stories that make up the work illustrates the theme of the claims of passion which collide with social imperatives.

However, whether Prévost's choice of the name Julie for his narrator's sister in the first book of the *Mémoires d'un homme de qualité* is a conscious recollection of Mme d'Aulnoy's heroine must remain an unanswerable question. As Pierre Fauchery has pointed out, Prévost was not alone amongst eighteenth-century novelists in choosing this name for his heroine.[24] In his creation of Julie, Prévost sketches out three themes to which he was to return in his later fiction: close brother and sister ties — Julie is the first object of the narrator's passionate adoration;[25] she is eminently an *âme sensible*; and she is doomed to die young, the victim of male passion (in her case, the presumed victim of male lust).

To accept that the shadow of Mme d'Aulnoy's heroine may be glimpsed behind Prévost's writing in the *Mémoires d'un homme de qualité* poses important questions about the nature of literary influence: what significance should be attached to a writer's use of literary themes or *topoi* in understanding and defining his or her work? In the case of Mme d'Aulnoy and Prévost, we see that the initial choice of name for the passionately loved sister-figure leads each writer in diametrically opposed directions. In the woman-authored text of 1690 the heroine is at the outset a clearly delineated figure, prepared to challenge society's unjust laws in the name of a mutual passion, whereas Prévost's Julie is a silent shadowy figure, representing a notion of women's victimhood which is in fundamental respects at variance with the Aulnoy model: the presumed victim of a bungled attempt at abduction, she is shot and fatally wounded at an early stage in the narrative.[26] She remains a voiceless, lifeless character, the prototype of the Prevostian heroine whose death is the consequence of men's passion.[27] Prévost's literary universe is a complex subject and far exceeds the confines of this article.[28] Put simply, a comparison of the two texts reveals important similarities as well as a fundamental difference. Prévost is indebted to a literary tradition of which Mme d'Aulnoy was a major exponent in his use of structural devices, in his conception of passion and the passionate hero, but his conception of female character and of female victimhood marks a radical divergence from the Aulnoy tradition. What is fundamentally lacking in Prévost's heroine is the subversive element which is a hallmark of Mme d'Aulnoy's presentation of her heroine. The notion of female victimhood, which, as a literary theme, had many avatars in the novel from Mme de Lafayette to Laclos, was by its very nature destined to be interpreted differently by men and women authors. One might say that Prévost wrote like a man and that Mme d'Aulnoy had written as a woman living in Ancien Regime France.

The character of Prévost's Julie, when read in parallel with Mme d'Aulnoy's's heroine, raises two further interrelated issues. The first is that of the unacknowledged debt of eighteenth-century novelists to their women predecessors. Although *La Princesse de Clèves* has been accepted into the canon of mainstream prose fiction, the question of her influence on the development of the eighteenth-century novel has been confined to the study of Nemours as the prototype of the seducer, in other words, her masterpiece is read as a masculine novel, so to speak.[29] The influence of the women novelists who succeeded her still remains for the most part uncharted territory. And yet, particularly with a novelist like Prévost, whose ardent imagination and predilection for *romanesque topoi* set him apart from other mainstream novelists of the period, the question of the presence in his writings of elements which have their origins in female literary tradition should be asked.

To compare Mme d'Aulnoy's Julie with the heroine of Rousseau's masterpiece may seem an act of *hubris* on my part. On the one hand we have a mere best-seller written by a long-forgotten woman writer and on the other, one of the most famous novels of the eighteenth century, written by a man of literary and philosophical genius. Moreover, *La Nouvelle Héloïse* must surely be one of the most minutely examined works of French prose fiction. And yet the question may still be asked: is there any discernible link between the two Julies? The first half of *La Nouvelle Héloïse* recounts the story of a passionate love between two young innocents, a love which is condemned by society, admittedly a literary *topos* which far predates Mme d'Aulnoy's text. It is however a *topos* whose precise emergence in the prose fiction of modern France is attributable to the work of those women writers who succeeded Mme de Lafayette whom I referred to at the beginning of this article, so that for the purposes of the immediate literary framework in which Rousseau was writing it was a feminine tradition.

Reading Rousseau's text in the light of this tradition sheds a new and at times amusing light on his intentions. The narrative structure of the first three parts of *La Nouvelle Héloïse* is much too familiar for me to rehearse it here. Read in the light of the feminine literary tradition that Mme d'Aulnoy played a key role in establishing, it takes on a somewhat different resonance. The lovers, Julie d'Etanges and the young Saint Preux are separated by social barriers, but amusingly Rousseau has inverted the *topos* of the girl being of humbler birth and therefore ineligible: it is Julie who is of higher social status and therefore inaccessible to her lover in the eyes of society. However, Rousseau's story of passion is also a debate on aspects of social morality. His Julie, although passionately in love with Saint Preux, has interiorized the moral code established by society. While acknowledging the existence of their love, she does not question the right of society to impose its laws. The anguish of moral conflict which co-exists with an overwhelming passion makes a powerful literary impact on readers more than two hundred years on. Writing of their love in Letter VII, Julie states: 'Jamais il ne forma d'union si parfaite: jamais il n'en forma de si durable'.[30] A love she contrasts with a morality which constrains her, as a woman, to adopt a mode of behaviour which she describes as: 'être fausse par devoir et mentir par modestie' (212). Julie's indictment of the young girl's lot sums up women's destiny as perceived by the women novelists of an earlier generation: 'On passe ainsi ses beaux jours sous la tirannie des bienséances, qu'aggrave enfin celle des parens dans un lien mal assorti' (212). When their separation seems inevitable Julie writes to her lover asserting the enduring nature of their mutual love:

> Oui mon ami, nous serons unis malgré notre éloignement: nous serons heureux en dépit du sort. C'est l'union des cœurs qui fait leur véritable félicité. (236)

This concept of 'l'union des cœurs' is modified significantly by Julie in the same letter to 'l'union des âmes'(237). What should one make of this apparent echo of the first Julie's ringing challenge to the injustice of social convention regarding marriage? I would not see it as a conscious echo on Rousseau's part, but rather as evidence of a literary heritage shared by writer and reader. The point is not to prove or disprove that Rousseau may have read Mme d'Aulnoy's text or that of any of her sister writers. The point is that his readers were certainly familiar with this now forgotten literature and the use Rousseau makes of this *topos* would therefore have a particular resonance for them which has been lost to us.

The theme of *l'union des cœurs*, one of the several elements in the complex dialectics of *La Nouvelle Héloïse*, illustrates the nature of the problem encoun-tered when trying to identify and assess the importance of women's contribution to the novel in the eighteenth century. On the one hand it is inconceivable that Julie and her sister heroines should have left no trace in the novel beyond the narrow confines of the feminine novel; the concept of first- and second-class literature is not one that bears close examination. On the other hand, the traces of this influence are immensely difficult to assess both because they appear in fundamentally modified form in the works of men novelists and, as I have suggested, because the precise nature of their contribution to the novel in the eighteenth century remains unrecognized. Mme d'Aulnoy's Julie and her kind are thus both a presence and an absence; the similarities between them and the heroines of Prévost and Rousseau serve to point up the fundamental differences. An understanding of this long-forgotten writing by women novelists, by enabling us to understand the specific quality of the feminine voice, enables us more clearly to define the masculine voice in the novel when it is heard in the context of an aesthetic tradition in which and against which it is seeking expression.[31]

It would be a truism to state that *La Nouvelle Héloïse* is not only a novel of passion but one of socialization: unlike Mme d'Aulnoy's Julie, Rousseau's heroine does not marry her lover; and in the second part of the story of Julie and Saint Preux, Rousseau has recourse to another *topos* of female fiction, that of the heroine being married off to a father-figure, a theme first poignantly exploited by Mme d'Aulnoy's sister novelist, Mlle Bernard in 1687 in *Eléonor d'Yvrée*.[32] As Joan Hinde Stewart has demonstrated, the theme of marriage to a (sexually unattractive) father-figure was one that haunted women's fiction throughout the eighteenth century,[33] and one that would have been familiar to Rousseau's readers in life as well as literature. In marrying his heroine off to a father-figure Rousseau is both challenging an established (feminine) literary tradition and stressing the triumph of socialization over passion. It was a message that would not be lost on readers brought up on the fictions of Mme d'Aulnoy's and her successors.

No work of literature, however great, can be viewed in isolation; all texts must be read in dialogue with others; Rousseau's masterpiece may in some respects be read as a counterblast to the values first preached by Mme d'Aulnoy's Julie.

UNIVERSITY COLLEGE LONDON

NOTES

1. Nancy K. Miller, *The Heroine's Text: Readings in the French and English Novel* (New York: Columbia University Press, 1980), pp. x–xi.

2. See for instance John Campbell, *Questions of Interpretation in 'La Princesse de Clèves'* (Amsterdam: Rodopi, 1996).

3. Catherine Bernard (1662–1712). Principal works of prose fiction: *Éléonor d'Yvrée* (1687), *Le Comte d'Amboise* (1689), *Inès de Cordoue* (1696).

4. Marie-Catherine d'Aulnoy (c. 1650–1705). Author of: *Histoire d'Hypolite, comte de Duglas* (1690); *Histoire de Jean de Bourbon, Prince de Carency* (1692); *Le Comte de Warwick* (1703). One of most successful writers of her day, in addition to these historical novels, she also wrote Travel Accounts and Historical Memoirs.

5. Charlotte-Rose Caumont de La Force (c. 1650–1724). She wrote five historical novels: *Histoire secrète de Bourgogne* (1694); *Histoire secrète de Henry IV, roy de Castille* (1695); *Histoire de Marguerite de Valois* (1696); *Gustave Vasa, histoire de Suède* (1697); *Anecdote galante ou histoire secrète de Cathérine de Bourbon* (1703).

6. See for instance Alain Niderst, *Fontenelle à la recherche de lui-même (1657–1702)* (Paris: Nizet, 1972); M.-T. Hipp, *Mythes et réalités: Enquête sur le roman et les mémoires (1660–1700)* (Paris: Klincksiek, 1976); F. Gevrey, *L'Illusion et ses procédés* (Paris: José Corti, 1988); Catherine Bernard, *Œuvres*, tome 1 *Romans et Nouvelles*, Textes établis, présentés et annotés par Franco Piva (Fasano & Paris: Schena-Nizet, 1993).

7. See Raymonde Robert, *Le conte de fées littéraire en France de la fin du XVIIᵉ à la fin du XVIIIᵉ siècle* (Nancy: Presses universitaires, 1981); Marina Warner, *From the Beast to the Blond* (London: Vintage, 1995).

8. For a discussion of the relationship between the status of the woman writer and the *conte de fée* as a literary genre see Lewis C. Seifert, *Les Fées modernes*: Women, Fairy Tales, and the Literary Field in Late Seventeenth-Century France, *Going Public, Women and Publishing in Early Modern France*, ed. by Elizabeth C. Goldsmith and Dena Goodman (Ithaca and London: Cornell University Press, 1995), 129–45.

9. Joan DeJean, 'Classical Reeducation: Decanonizing the Feminine', in *Displacements: Women, Tradition, Literatures in French*, ed. by Joan DeJean & Nancy K. Miller (Baltimore and London: Johns Hopkins University Press, 1991), pp. 22–36.

10. More than forty editions of the *Histoire d'Hypolite* appeared during the course of the eighteenth and nineteenth centuries. English translations began to appear shortly after the novel was first published in France. All references to the text are given from the following edition: Madame d'Aulnoy, *L'Histoire d'Hypolite, comte de Duglas*, ed. with an introduction in English and French by Shirley Jones Day (London: Institute of Romance Studies, 1994).

11. Madame de Lafayette, *Romans et nouvelles*, ed. by E. Magne, with an introduction by
     A. Niderst (Paris, Éditions Garnier, 1970), p. 247.

12. In creating her heroine, Mme d'Aulnoy was clearly influenced by Mlle Bernard's
     Éléonor d'Yvrée, whose heroine, Éléonor, the orphaned daughter of a political exile,
     is prevented from marrying the duc de Misnie by her lack of social status and dowry.
     These givens, which play a subordinate role in Mlle Bernard's text, are of primary
     importance in Mme d'Aulnoy's account.

13. For a discussion of the very different function of money in the masculine novel, see
     English Showalter, *The Evolution of the French Novel 1641–1782* (Princeton: Princeton
     University Press, 1972), pp. 224–34.

14. 'Mais les hommes conservent-ils de la passion dans ces engagements éternels?'
     Lafayette, *Romans et nouvelles*, p. 387.

15. Of Mme de Chartres's moral teaching to her daughter we read that: 'elle lui faisait
     voir [...] quelle tranquillité suivait la vie d'une honnête femme'(248); and happiness is
     precisely defined: 'ce qui seul peut faire le bonheur d'une femme, qui est d'aimer son
     mari et d'en être aimée.' Lafayette, *Romans et nouvelles*, p. 248.

16.

    > chaque jour, chaque instant je sens ajoûter de nouvelles peines à mes peines,
    > [...] les reproches secrets que l'on se fait à soy-même, les remords qui suivent
    > le tendre souvenir d'un Amant encore aimé, le désir de faire son devoir &
    > d'arracher de son cœur une inclination qui n'y plus estre sans crime. (76)

17. Olwen Hufton, *The Prospect Before Her: A History of Women in Western Europe,
     Volume One 1500–1800* (London: Harper Collins, 1995), pp. 251–98.

18. It should be noted in passing that the first *conte de fée* to be published, *L'Ile de la
     Félicité*, appeared in the text of the *Histoire d'Hypolite*.

19. It is as a successful seducer that Nemours is introduced to us (Lafayette, *Romans et
     nouvelles*, p. 244) This factor is of crucial importance in the development of Mme de
     Clèves's relationship with him. Of her attempt to hide her passion we read, 'Un
     homme moins pénétrant que lui ne s'en fût peut-être pas aperçu; mais il avait déjà été
     aimé tant de fois [...].' (298).

20. See Joan DeJean, *Displacements*, pp. 30–31.

21. Georges May's statement, made over thirty years ago, that the history of the
     eighteenth-century novel still remained to be written, sadly still holds good for
     women's contribution to its history. Their place in its history is still to be identified
     and acknowledged. This is particularly true of the period prior to Mme de Tencin.
     (*Le Dilemme du roman au XVIII᷎ siècle: Etude sur les rapports du roman et de la critique*

(1715-1761) (New Haven, CT: Yale University Press, Paris: Presses Universitaires de France, 1963), p. 1.)

22. *Mémoires et Aventures d'un Homme de qualité qui s'est retiré du monde* (1728–31).

23. See *Œuvres de Prévost*, I, *Mémoires et aventures d'un homme de qualité qui s'est retiré du monde, Histoire du chevalier des Grieux et de Manon Lescaut,* texte établi par Pierre Berthiaume et Jean Sgard, (Grenoble: Presses Universitaires de Grenoble, 1978). The narrative in the first five books, which contains the plot Renoncour's account of his unhappy love for Selime makes liberal use of the *topoi* of the hero being taken into captivity, his being smuggled into the harem where he wins the heroine's love, his carrying her off and marrying her. In his excellent general study of the novel prior to 1789, Henri Coulet describes this kind of writing, in his discussion of Mme d'Aulnoy as 'le goût d'un romanesque facile', *Le roman jusqu'à la Révolution* (Paris: Armand Colin, 1967), p. 291.

24. Pierre Fauchery, *La Destinée féminine dans le roman européen du dix-huitième siècle 1713-1807; Essai de gynémythie romanesque* (Paris, Armand Colin, 1972) p. 70, cit. *Œuvres de Prévost*, VIII, *Commentaires et notes*, p. 234.

25. Prévost's third major novel, *Le Doyen de Killerine* (1735–40), is based on the relationship between the narrator and his brothers and sisters.

26. Her story occupies a mere six pages in Renoncour's account of his life, which unfolds over 114 pages.

27. She is allowed to speak for the first time on the eve of her death, when her indifference to the joys of this world and her willingness to die are quoted at length. In the same vein of *sensibilité*, her final words are reported:

> Je suis blessée mortellement [...] c'est Dieu qui me sauve l'honneur [...] n'oubliez jamais une sœur qui vous aimera plus que soi-même. (24)

28. Prévost's literary art and its inspiration forms the subject of a masterly study by Jean Sgard, *Prévost romancier* (Paris: Corti, 1968).

29. On the influence of Nemours as the prototype of the seducer in the eighteenth-century novel, see Laurent Versini, *Laclos et la tradition: Essai sur les sources et la technique des 'Liaisons dangereuses'* (Paris: Klincksieck, 1968), pp. 118, 165.

30. Jean-Jacques Rousseau, *Œuvres complètes* II (Paris, Gallimard, Bibliothèque de la Pléiade, 1961), seconde partie, p. 212.

31. For a discussion of the importance of understanding the inter-relationship of men's and women's writing in the eighteenth-century novel in France, see Nancy K. Miller, 'Men's Reading, Women's Writing: Gender and the Rise of the Novel', in *Displacements: Women, Tradition, Literatures in French*, ed. By Joan DeJean & Nancy K.

Miller (Baltimore and London: John Hopkins University Press, 1991), pp. 38–54 (pp. 42–48).

32.   Eléonor is forced to marry the elderly comte de Retelois by her father to repay a debt of honour.

33.   Joan Hinde Stewart, *Gynographs: French Novels by Women of the Late Eighteenth Century* (Lincoln & London: University of Nebraska Press, 1993), pp. 152–70.

JUDITH BEALE

Angel or Sylph?
The two-faced woman in *Les Illustres Françaises*

In the eighteenth century, 'an idea called "woman"' may be seen as the Leading Lady in the Story of Story, the development of the novel.[1] This is a study of two of Robert Challe's '*illustres Françaises*', Angélique de Contamine and Silvie des Frans, viewed as one woman with two faces. Marked parallels in the initial presentation of these two characters justify this identification, which throws light upon the significance of their very different fates and authorial evaluations.

1.   Parallels
The parallel starts, quite formally, with their names. The work consists of the stories of seven young couples, within a frame-narrative. Five of these stories identify their subjects by their family names: 'Histoire de M. X et de Mlle Y'. The others (the second and sixth) identify the two women only by their given names: Angélique and Silvie. This already signals some shared difference between them and the other young women whose stories are recounted.

   Moreover, the names of these two women have semantic content. The significance of 'Angélique' is obvious: she is named for a higher, more godlike order of being, with connotations of both moral goodness and sweetness of temper; but also, since angels are spiritual beings, lack of passion. 'Silvie', by contrast, suggests a silvan, woodland or wild creature: le Grand Larousse gives 'wood anemone' as one of the meanings of the word, while Littré gives a bird (*fauvette*). 'Sylph' provides a further resonance, since its feminine in French is *sylphide* — phonetically close to 'Silvie'. The Shorter Oxford English Dictionary dates the word 'sylph' from the mid-seventeenth century, giving two meanings: 'any of a race of elemental beings or spirits of the air', and 'a slender graceful woman or girl'. Shakespeare's Ariel is, in French, *un sylphe*.[2] Neither '*sylph*' nor '*sylphide*' appear in Furetière, but Littré records 17th century occurrences of both. The primary meaning given is 'prétendus génies élémentaires de l'air', but the citations produce two further meanings for the feminine form. Littré says: 'On dit en parlant d'une jeune femme élancée et gracieuse: C'est une sylphide, elle danse comme une sylphide'. Robert adds 'Avoir une taille de sylphide, très mince', attributing this to the *Académie*. Finally, Robert gives 'créature fémi-nine de rêve, fille de l'imagination'; and both dictionaries give a telling quota-tion from Rousseau, a passage in the *Confessions* concerning the wide-spread belief that *la Nouvelle Héloïse* was autobiographical:

> [...] on était loin de concevoir à quel point je puis m'enflammer pour des êtres
> imaginaires. Sans quelques réminiscences de jeunesse et Madame d'Houdetot,
> les amours que j'ai sentis et décrits n'auraient été qu'avec des Sylphides.[3]

Thus, Silvie's name gives us connotations of wildness, slender grace, and dream-like unreality. She is described as 'si menue que je la prenais facilement entre mes mains' (310),[4] she sings and plays perfectly (a hint of the siren, perhaps), and her dancing is bewitching; three hours in her company seem but a moment gone (314–15).

Challe, in his *Préface*, comments on '[l]es noms dérivés de ceux de bap-tême que j'ai donnés à mes héroïnes, tels que Manon, Babet, et d'autres' (7); but Angélique and Silvie are not among them.[5] By contrast with the cosy, domesti-cated diminutives of the other young women, these two are signalled as 'other', as outsiders, outwith the social or even the human norm.

Indeed, Angélique and Silvie do, expressly, share the quality of being socially impossible. Angélique's father was technically an aristocrat, but the family has lost caste: he was 'cadet des cadets, n'ayant que la cape et l'épée' (83), married beneath him, espoused a losing cause, and lost his life; his destitute wife was forced into service. Angélique herself, taken into a noble household out of charity, is taught to read and write in order to do the household accounts, subsequently becoming companion to Mlle de Vougy. She is granted a maiden name, but it is only mentioned once (112). Though she acquires aristocratic polish, her mother remains socially unacceptable:

son esprit [...] ne pouvait être fort poli, n'ayant jamais vu que des paysans en
province, ou des gens du tiers état à Paris. (109)

Throughout their courtship, the financial aristocrat Contamine addresses her
patronisingly, first as 'ma belle fille', then as 'belle Angélique'. He says

serais-je excusable dans le monde, si je vous épousais telle que vous êtes? [...]
épargnez-moi la honte d'une si grande chute. (96)

to which Angélique's spirited response is that of the Pretty Maid in the old
song:

Nobody asked you, Sir, she said. (97)

Silvie is, if anything, in worse case: she has no family name. Nor, though
she marries Des Frans, is she ever referred to by his name. Taken from an or-
phanage into a noble household, she passes as *un enfant trouvé*. She understands
herself to be the illegitimate daughter of the Duc de Buringes and his mother's
demoiselle, but she makes a mystery of her birth, which upon its revelation she
describes as 'une naissance que les lois ont déclarée infâme' (355). When, against
her wishes, Des Frans persists in his hunt for her origins, she resorts to bribery
to construct a false identity as the daughter of an impoverished (and, as it turns
out, thoroughly disreputable) gentleman. Her mitigation includes the curious
claim that this piece of trickery was bound to fail in any event, since Des Frans
could have looked up her name on the birth register signed when they first met
as godparents of an orphan (354); but as the editors suggest, since her parentage
was such a secret it is unlikely that she was then calling herself Silvie de Buringe
(377). Yet even her own belief turns out to be false: her mother was not a *suivante*, but a 'fille de grande qualité' who was forced to marry another (390). Des
Frans' mother refuses to recognise Silvie as her daughter-in-law, because the
story of her birth is too incredible, and what is more, she cannot be trusted:

Cette fourbe était trop bien concertée pour la faire passer pour un coup de jeunesse. A mon égard, un esprit si subtil [another echo of the 'spirits of the air'?] me paraît dangereux et me fait peur. C'est à mon sens en savoir trop, et en entreprendre trop pour une fille qui n'a pas vingt ans. [...] Je ne vivrais pas en repos avec un esprit si intrigant. (402)

Angélique is outcast by poverty and loss of caste; Silvie by suspicion and uncertainty about 'who she is', made worse rather than better by her attempts to compensate for it. Wealth, too, paradoxically casts a cloud over both, since it appears unticketed by any respectable source. Silvie cannot show her riches to be a legitimate inheritance (and of course they are not, though they come from her father); Angélique's sudden and unexplained magnificence immediately calls her chastity in question (114–15). For both of them, the obstacle to their union with the young man of their choice is his mother, and his inability or refusal even to attempt to gain his mother's consent to the unorthodox match. The couples' different responses to this obstacle (acceptance and defiance) play no small part in their different fates.

And because they lack socially acceptable family, the two young women are socially vulnerable. They have no legitimate protectors or patrons: one false move, one misinterpreted event, can destroy them. They are at the mercy of inference from appearances and rumour; they have no social substance. Both, while living in isolation — itself a suspicious circumstance — prudently surround themselves with respectable bourgeoises (111, 317), but it is a fragile protection, as Silvie's story shows: her secret husband's insistence that she receive male as well as female company (406) renders her 'fair game' to male aggression, and so victim of that same husband's rage.

2.   Contrasts

Nancy K. Miller divides *The Heroine's Text* into two Parts: 'The Euphoric Text' and 'The Dysphoric Text'. Among the euphoric texts are *La Vie de Marianne* (1731) (Chapter 2: 'The Virtuous Orphan') and *Pamela* (1740) (Chapter 3: 'The Rewards of Virtue'); among the dysphoric, *Manon Lescaut* (1731) (Chapter 5: 'Love for a Harlot'), and *Clarissa* (1747–48) (Chapter 6: 'The Misfortunes of

Virtue: I'). The stories of Angélique and Silvie fall neatly into this classification. Although Angélique, unlike Marianne, has identifiable parents, they are no part of *le monde* to which both young women aspire. Both, poor and subaltern, decline wealth, comfort and elevation to the *demi-monde*, out of ambition to join the real thing: they gamble against huge odds for the ultimate prize, and win. As does Pamela; she differs from Marianne and Angélique in accepting that she does not, in essence, belong to it. Pamela is elevated; Marianne and Angélique are recognized. While Pamela insists on her humble origins and status, opposing her lower-class virtue to aristocratic vice, Marianne (unconstrained by any known parentage) claims a nobility of essence.[6] Though more akin to Marianne than to Pamela, Angélique is able to preserve more modesty on this subject, by the simple expedient of third-person rather than first-person narration: she can (in Pamela's tone) treat her aristocratic *amant* to lessons in *noblesse oblige* on account of her lowly status (87–88), while being credited by her narrator with 'toutes les manières nobles, et l'air d'une fille de qualité' (109). All three, however, are dealt with in the same manner by the male hegemony: an initial condescending move to seduce a supposedly-dazzled inferior; ruffled feathers on frustration; an ensuing offer of 'contract' to establish and maintain as mistress; more ruffled feathers, culminating in an eventual offer of marriage and high social position.[7] Moreover, all three oppose the same strategy to this male campaign: an obstinate claim to (at least) the same virtue as gentlefolk; manipulation from below; appeals to the pathetic (designed to engage the Reader as ally long before it seduces the Seducer); holding out for 'deserved' worldly success, or Virtue Rewarded.

The dysphoric heroines, Silvie, Manon and Clarissa, have less obviously in common. Yet the dysphoric trajectory is clear: all three become, according to the Code, 'fallen women'; all three die; all three are loved/desired to desperation and despair. Only in the case of Clarissa is this trajectory perfected: morally Immaculata, her Evil Seducer and her Despairing Lover are one; he also dies. Clarissa is generally accredited as exceptional from the beginning,[8] but Manon and Silvie so strike the percipient observer. Manon's appearance and demeanour 'étaient si peu conformes à sa condition, qu'en tout autre état je l'eusse prise pour une princesse'.[9] Silvie 'me rendit mon salut fort civilement, et

me parla si juste, que je ne doutai pas que ce ne fût une fille hors du commun';
she shows signs of 'le commerce des gens de la première qualité' (308, 310). But
it is in their fates that they most resemble one another, especially Silvie and
Clarissa.[10] All three are duelled over; but while Manon dies fleeing with her
lover from the consequences, Silvie and Clarissa are victims of drugging, rape,
imprisonment, and humiliation moral and physical. It kills them both. Their
natural protectors — Clarissa's father, Silvie's husband — abandon them, then
condemn them for the results.

It is no coincidence that the frame-narrative treats Angélique quite
differently from Silvie. The frame of the seven *histoires* consists of a group of
friends, increasing from two to twelve, who gather in private to tell, hear and
discuss their various stories. It is society in microcosm, performing a role of
sharing, integration and socialisation; and a form of exorcism-by-exclusion of the
socially dangerous and disruptive. Angélique, now Madame de Contamine,
dominates the frame group. She is introduced early as 'une dame d'une magnificence achevée' (74), and immediately identified as the former *suivante*. She
authorises the telling of her story to explain how this transformation came
about. Thereafter, she is the frame group's moral and social authority, and in
particular controls and rebukes Des Frans's anti-feminist sniping, his persistence
in denigrating all women on the basis of Silvie's misconduct. Silvie herself, by
contrast, is absent from the frame; she is dead (16), so whatever the group's
ultimate verdict upon her, she cannot be integrated or accepted into it. Her
voice, however, does speak once in the frame, between the two versions of her
story: the sixth, told by Des Frans, and the seventh, told by Dupuis. Following
Des Frans's narration, Dupuis reads to the company the letter which Silvie wrote
from her convent to Gallouin, her seducer (431–33); the group then comes close
to quarrelling over the correct moral evaluation of Silvie, some pitying and some
despising her, and have to break off in order to recover their tempers (435). Thus
not only is Silvie excluded from the group; even in death, she is a source of
disruption within it. The role of the dysphoric is to provide shading for the
euphoric, darkness to make the bright shine brighter.

Underlying these textual contrasts are deeper and more archetypal contrasts: these two *personnages* are loaded with fairy-tale motifs and evocations,

darkness v light on a different level. Angélique's is the story of Cinderella, complete with transformation and fairy godmother. Like Cinderella, she is socially invisible in her lowly status (74). She is transformed into unrecognisable magnificence; indeed, the transformation-theme introduces her to the text, and motivates the telling of her story. It is emphasised as quasi-magical or miraculous:

> Est-il possible, Madame, [...] que ce soit vous que j'ai vue autrefois si différente
> de vous-même?; [...] Je vous avoue que c'est un changement qui me passe, et
> que je ne puis presque comprendre. (74–75)

The surface transformation in her story itself is nearly her undoing, since the Princesse de Coligny ascribes it to 'la débauche' (114–15); but it leads the Princess to play fairy godmother, completing the surface transformation with a social one, enabling the poor *suivante* to marry her Prince. The Princess waves the wand of her social position and moral authority, makes Angélique shine in *le monde* as Cinderella did at the ball, and fits her into society as Cinderella's foot fitted the glass slipper. Manon Dupuis presents Angélique to Des Frans with a kind of Cinderella *moralité*: 'Madame [...] ne doit à présent sa fortune qu'à sa beauté et à sa vertu' (75). But we might also apply the *moralité* which Perrault provides for his *Cendrillon*: intelligence, courage, birth, good sense, are no use

> Si vous n'avez, pour les faire valoir
> Ou des parrains ou des marraines.[11]

Silvie, by contrast, is the type of the wild mythical fairy-woman of the woods recalled by Keats:

> I met a lady in the meads
> Full beautiful, a faery's child;
> Her hair was long, her foot was light,
> And her eyes were wild.

She enchants him with 'a faery's song', then abandons him to wake alone 'on the cold hill side'.[12] Whether she herself is benevolent or malevolent, the love of such a creature is always malign for mortal men. As René Démoris has pointed out, the moral vindication of Silvie 'ne change que l'interprétation de son histoire, non cette histoire elle-même'.[13] The man who loves her is lost to human society and the love of women. Des Frans spends seven years in exile because of Silvie; he says despairingly to his friend Des Ronais, '[V]ous savez à présent mon histoire, me conseillez-vous encore de me remarier?' Yes, says Des Ronais, 'pour la tranquillité de votre vie' (436) — a partial recuperation only.

By contrast with Angélique, who is 'une petite personne' (85), Silvie despite her slenderness is taller than average (310); and compared with the defensive and evasive strategies adopted by Angélique, a much more decisive and active personality. But the most striking of her fairy-tale attributes is her hair.[14] There is a hierarchy of hair in *Les Illustres Françaises*. The five women who are both chaste and successful are not endowed with hair worth mentioning. Babet Fenouil and la Veuve have black hair (187, 515); they sin against chastity, though the text approves them for their generosity and constancy to their men. Only in the two dysphoric texts is the heroine's hair emphasised and celebrated. Marie-Madeleine de l'Épine has 'les cheveux du plus beau blond clair qu'on puisse voir au monde' (224); her blondness is referred to twice thereafter. Silvie's hair is even more egregious: 'Ses cheveux étaient plus longs qu'elle d'un grand pied, annelés, et du plus beau chatain qu'on puisse voir' (310). She has to stand on a table to have it combed; the length of her hair is possible only in fairy-tale, as Michèle Weil points out in her excellent book.[15] Moreover, this hair plays a significant role on two occasions. First, when Des Frans goes to abuse her after hearing much to her disadvantage, she falls at his feet in tears; she is dressed, or rather undressed, for bed, her robe falls open, her long loose hair falls around her, covering her completely. Des Frans is overcome: 'Elle me parut une seconde Madeleine' (335). The biblical reference is striking,[16] but with it comes a more ominous one. The immediately preceding story was that of Marie-Madeleine de l'Épine, who was insulted, brutalised, abandoned and banished to a lonely and horrible death in the poor-house. This textual association of Silvie with the unfortunate Marie-Madeleine comes to fruition in the second incident involving Silvie's hair. Des Frans, having found her in bed with Gallouin, lures her from Paris, and imprisons her in a burnt-out ruin. 'Je la fis déshabiller, je l'obligeai à se couper elle-même les cheveux que je brûlai en sa présence à une chandelle' — again, myth has overcome *vraisemblance*. 'Je les regrette encore: je n'en ai vu de ma vie de plus beaux, ni de plus longs, ni en plus grande quantité' (416). He is afraid of her power to enchant him, so he destroys its source, in a reversal of Samson and Delilah.

Des Frans hints at supernatural forces in his account of his relations with Silvie, going far beyond conventional references to womanly 'charms'. He is bewitched, dragged under, obsessed, feverish, confused, weakened and out of control (312, 357, 324, 335). Silvie intends him no harm, but is aware of her effect. She gives him the fairy warning: I'm dangerous to you, keep away or you will regret it (317, 356). Twice she tells him 'rendez-vous à vous-même' (317, 356), adding poignancy to his words to Des Ronais on his eventual return from exile: 'je me rends à mes amis, à mes parents, et à moi-même [...]' (10).

Nor should we forget the magic of which Silvie herself is victim, unparalleled elsewhere in the text — her *collier*, filched and rendered aphrodisiac by Gallouin. It is not a love-charm in the emotional sense, but a spell which produces irresistible, devouring carnal desire; Gallouin himself is shocked at its bizarre effect (546). Moreover, the necklace's mysteries are not exhausted by its effects on Silvie. Des Frans takes it from her neck as she sleeps with Gallouin, thereby undoing the spell, but causing Gallouin to suspect that the devil himself has made mischief (549). Silvie is deeply enmeshed in the supernatural and other-worldly, both exerting and suffering 'une puissance plus forte que la nature' (15).

She is done to death by the combined brutalities of two men; but from the social perspective, she is responsible for their destruction. Both become exiles from their society; Gallouin suffers the unlikely death predicted for him, while for Des Frans, Silvie and Gallouin '[...] m'ont fait regarder ma patrie comme mon enfer' (16). Silvie's moral status may affect audience sympathies; but it does not make her safe for society.

3.   Worldliness

We must now ask to what purpose the resonances of fairy tale are being in-voked. My suggested answer is: in the service of worldliness, the attachment of 'primary or even exclusive importance to ordered social existence, to life within a public system of values and gestures', in an 'ethos and literature [which] can arise only when society becomes an object of conscious cultivation, when it asserts outward closure and inward publicity' as Peter Brooks puts it. Challe's work may be seen as an extended sequence of *portraits moraux,* which Brooks characterises as 'the expression of a total public act of knowing by one person of another'.[17] Silvie's *portrait* is incoherent, self-contradictory and incomprehensible (311-12). Since she is unknowable, no clear evaluation of her is possible, and the attempt, as already noted, causes anger and dispute among the frame-group (433-35), as well as a curt rebuke from Contamine to his wife (551). Silvie would endanger this fragile society. She is beyond the pale, the 'out-ward closure'; only her death enables them to weep over her, bury her in the dark, and re-integrate Des Frans by marrying him off to another woman. The formerly invisible Angélique, by contrast, emerges into the full light of social day.

One unifying theme running through the work is the recuperation of Des Frans as a social being. He enters the text isolated, threatened by society; it relents, opens to let him in, and calls him by name, recognising him (9-10). He is one of only two people present at every narration. He takes on social respon-sibility, helping to reconcile Des Ronais and Manon Dupuis, and to bring Jussy and Babet Fenouil safely to the altar. Angélique's Cinderella-story is a *moralité* for him, rebuking his initial incredulity by showing him what might have been, had he bent his own arrogant neck to society's yoke. Angélique herself harasses, shames and manipulates him throughout the work towards civilised behaviour and the taming bond of arranged marriage.

The ideology of *Les Illustres Françaises* does not propose female chastity, or the 'fetish' of virginity, as its prime value. The fallen virgin, Babet Fenouil, is forgiven and praised by the authoritative Angélique (216); la Veuve, Dupuis's long-term lover, is treated sympathetically (506-35). Both are allowed happi-ness. What the work condemns utterly, and punishes with death, is *secret mar-*

riage, the violation of that 'inward publicity' on which society depends. Angélique's judgment on Marie-Madeleine and Des Prez allows no credit to the solemnity and sincerity of their marriage ceremony:

> presque toutes ces sortes de mariages faits à l'insu ou malgré les parents, ne sont jamais heureux. M. Des Prez en est une preuve vivante par sa douleur éternelle. (289)

The living man, we note, is the proof, not the dead woman; women are instruments of social good or ill, but a man lost to society impoverishes it. Marriage is not a private matter between two people and their god, as Marie-Madeleine thought (251). It is a social matter, the scaffolding of society, the fence against 'désordre' (295), and as such must be public.

We may contrast the the outcomes of two other parallel tales, Terny/ Bernay (third) and Jussy/Fenouil (fourth). In both cases, crisis requires action, and the women demand elopement, blackmailing their unwilling men with suicide threats. Terny, resourceful and powerfully befriended, stages an unorthodox but public marriage by hijacking Clémence's profession as a nun (substituting himself for Christ as the bridegroom). The less adroit Jussy condemns himself even as he prepares to obey:

> [C]e n'était point un crime digne de mort que de faire des enfants; mais [...] le rapt en était un qui ne s'était jamais pardonné. (199)

It was pardoned, but only after a seven-year penance — and, crucially, because it failed.

The two lovers of Angélique and Silvie respond differently to the maternal obstacle. Contamine uses it to try to get his way *sans sacrement;* but when Angélique will have none of this, he resigns himself to patience. When the Princesse de Coligny proposes to speak for the marriage, he becomes even more scrupulous. Knowing that his mother cannot refuse the Princess, he confesses and renounces his love: 'tout le bon fils fit taire l'amant' (131). He has his priorities right, and is rewarded by maternal approval, enabling Angélique to be publicly married from the Princess's house into a blaze of righteousness, riches, rank and honour. Des Frans, by contrast, tolerates no impediment to his passions, whether love, desire, rage or vengeance. He lurches between infatuation and loathing, acting impetuously and self-defeatingly on each. He marries Silvie at midnight (385), in secret, despite 'des répugnances terribles' (377); he then compounds his insult to society by pretending to the hand of another woman (405), a false cloak of availability and engagement which his fate and his friends bring only too true (588). Marie-Madeleine comes to grief by a series of romantic coincidences, but Silvie's downfall is rooted in the nature of secret marriage itself. She makes the same fundamental error as Marie-Madeleine: '[...] de toute votre famille je ne veux épouser que vous' (377). She is even foolishly excited by the idea: 'En gardant le secret, outre les plaisirs du mariage, nous aurons encore ceux du mystère' (404). She and Des Frans do not acknowledge society's demand for publicity of its structural relationships. She has hidden and falsified her family origins; she agrees to hide and falsify her marriage. She is ruined because her seducer does not know that she is his friend's wife. Gallouin's ignorance of what should have been public knowledge enables the little society to pity him, and Des Frans to forgive him. The grievous wrong he did Silvie is given much less significance — save by Angélique, who is rebuked for it by her husband (551). By making a secret marriage, Des Frans has not incorporated the *sylphide* into society, but put himself outside it — as with the knight-at-arms, his heart is turned to stone. It is a hollow man who is re-integrated.

4.   *Two-faced woman, two-faced author*

Silvie is condemned as two-faced by Des Frans (311–12) and Contamine (433–34), and Madame Des Frans, who no doubt speaks for them all when she says '[J]e ne vivrais pas en repos avec un esprit si intrigant' (402). It is for the sake of their own tranquillity, and the taming of Des Frans, that the group needs to agree on her position in their collective history. Angélique herself does not entirely escape the suspicion of being a covert schemer, tinged though it is with admiration for her prudence and cleverness (85, 93, 96). But there can be no doubt that she, unlike Silvie, is approved by the work's official ideology. It would be anachronistic to suggest that the text is denigrating her for her prudence and caution, or her lack of romantic authenticity. The eighteenth century was an age which optimistically allied virtue and reason; virtue and self-interest were closely linked, indeed often equated. Angélique uses her beauty and her wits to best advantage, but in her circumstances that is simple common sense; her greatest achievement, the text suggests, was keeping her head: 'Cette lettre était d'un style à lui faire tout espérer, pourvu qu'elle sût se bien ménager; elle ne s'oublia pas' (96). The text rewards her with worldly blessings, and if there is a suggestion of *post hoc ergo propter hoc,* a hint that her success was more good management than good luck, this is more credit than discredit to one whose face is her fortune. If Angélique and Silvie are, in conception, alternative aspects of one woman-type, the Angélique-face smiles upon the future, while the Silvie-face weeps over the past.

Nevertheless, it is impossible to escape the suspicion that Challe himself was, at least to some extent, out of sympathy with the message of his own text, with its allocation of prizes and punishments. Angélique-or-Virtue-Rewarded frequently comes across as bossy, waspish and smug; the compliments paid to her by her associates sometimes feel rather laboured. By contrast, the writing of Silvie, tried, condemned and executed though she is, abounds with gracious and affectionate touches. The text's attitude to her ensnaring beauty is, as so often, ambivalent; but it is made clear that her grace and charm, her independence and wit, make her company a joy. Challe loads the text with convincing propaganda for public, socially acceptable marriage, and against '*désordre*'; yet the same text makes the non-conforming Silvie utterly irresistible — as, to a lesser extent, la Veuve; the two *personnages* most of us — surely including Challe himself — would choose to spend our time with. Perhaps he, like many another male writer (and most notably Rousseau), pays for the freedom to write his personal *sylphide* with her life.

BIRKBECK COLLEGE, LONDON

NOTES

1.   See Nancy K. Miller: *The Heroine's Text* (New York: Columbia University Press, 1980), p. ix.

2.
      Je suis l'enfant de l'air, un sylphe, moins qu'un rêve
      [...] Diaphane habitant de l'invisible éther.

      Hugo, *Odes et Ballades* II; see entries in Littré and Robert.

3.   Rousseau: *Confessions* xi, *Œuvres complètes* (Paris: Gallimard, 1959), vol I, 548.

4.   All references to *Les Illustres Françaises* are to the 1991 edition published by Droz (Geneva), ed. by Frédéric Deloffre and Jacques Cormier.

5.   There is one other exception, Clémence de Bernay, but I have found no relevant interpretative significance for this name. She is in need of mercy, but no more than several of the others.

6.   e.g. 'Etaient-elles [sc. mes délicatesses] dans mon sang? cela se pourrait bien [...]': Marivaux: *La Vie de Marianne*, ed. by Frédéric Deloffre (Paris: Classiques Garnier, 1963), p. 33.

7.   In Marianne's case, unlike the other two, the male role is split between Climal and Valville; but this hardly affects the basic structure (and Valville's flightiness suggests a Climal alter ego).

8.   Within the first sentence of the work, she is described by her friend Anna Howe as 'a young lady, whose distinguished merits have made her the public care [...]' and later in the first letter as 'excelling all her sex'. More tellingly even: 'Every eye [...] is upon you with the expectation of an example'. Richardson: *Clarissa or, the History of a Young Lady* (1747–78), ed. by Angus Ross (Harmondsworth: Viking Penguin, 1985), pp. 39–40.

9.   Prévost: *Histoire de Chevalier des Grieux et de Manon Lescaut*, ed. by Frédéric Deloffre (Paris: Classiques Garnier, 1990), p. 12, 1731 text.

10.   Richardson is thought to have been influenced by Challe; *Les Illustres Françaises* appeared in English as *Illustrious French Lovers* in 1727. See Jean Sgard, 'Challe et Prévost', in *Séminaire Robert Challe: Les Illustres Françaises*, ed. by Michèle Weil-Bergougnoux (Montpellier: Université Paul Valéry, 1995), pp. 119–27 (pp. 119, 120).

11.   Perrault, *Contes*, ed. by J.-P. Collinet (Paris: Folio, 1981), p. 178.

12.   Keats: *La Belle Dame sans Merci.*

13.   René Démoris: *Le Roman à la première Personne* (Paris: A. Colin, 1975), p. 309.

14.   Marina Warner devotes two chapters to the subject of hair in *From the Beast to the Blond* (London: Chatto & Windus), chapters 21 and 22.

15.   *Robert Challe Romancier* (Geneva: Droz, 1991), p. 94.

16. Luke 7:37–38; the identification of the woman as Mary Magdalen is legendary, though contradicted by John 11:2.

17. Peter Brooks: *The Novel of Worldliness* (Princeton: Princeton University Press, 1969), pp. 4, 5, 14.

RENÉ DÉMORIS

Parole de femme dans *les Egarements du cœur et de l'esprit*, de Crébillon fils

Une fois refermé le volume des *Egarements*, le lecteur ne saurait manquer de rêver sur l'extraordinaire figure féminine inventée par Crébillon, cette Mme de Lursay qui connaît, à la fin du livre, une étonnante assomption liée à un changement de régime du texte, magistralement analysé par un article inspiré de Michel Gilot[1]. Sans doute le narrateur nous apprend, aussitôt après l'extase, qu'en réalité, il ne l'aimait pas (aveu sans conséquence qui n'empêche pas de nouveaux plaisirs et l'acceptation d'un rendez-vous pour le lendemain) Cela ne compromet pas le triomphe du personnage et de l'énonciation féminine: car le narrateur, au discours qu'elle a tenu et où elle lui a raconté leur histoire, ne trouve rien à ajouter ou à corriger. A ce moment, Mme de Lursay confisque à Meilcour son rôle de narrateur, réduisant au silence non seulement le héros (la circonstance le justifie, il vient de se ridiculiser en lui supposant un amant dans quelque placard...), mais aussi le narrateur en titre. Silence double, dont le second importe davantage: c'est au sens fort du terme que Mme de Lursay *prend la parole* à son partenaire, dans un discours qui répond pleinement à toutes les questions qu'a pu se poser le lecteur au cours du roman: de ce point de vue, donc, une parole vraie, ce que semble reconnaître le silence du narrateur en titre. C'est dans le roman la signification de cette substitution énonciative que je tenterai d'analyser.

Le trait en effet mérite d'être relevé: il est inhabituel dans les romans-mémoires, et au moins surprenant dans un texte qui commence par un procès fait aux femmes. Cet écart entre un point de départ et un point d'arrivée, j'entreprends de l'analyser, pour tâcher de déterminer ce qu'a été le projet romanesque (à entendre par là l'intention consciente, et aussi une visée qui peut l'être moins) de Crébillon, spécialiste, jusque là, avec les *Lettres de la Marquise*, d'une écriture féminine non narrative, emboîtant le pas, avec les *Egarements*, à Prévost et

Marivaux: en 1736, il avait pu lire *Manon, le Paysan Parvenu*, deux ou trois parties de *La Vie de Marianne*, les *Mémoires d'un homme de qualité*, (son texte en porte des traces), qui avaient déjà donné quelques échantillons des ressources complexes de l'écriture à la première personne, en appelant à une lecture critique tenant compte de la position intéressée du narrateur, dans une entreprise qui a souvent caractère d'apologie[2].

C'est un homme qui écrit

L'énonciation primaire, dans les *Egarements*, on le sait, est masculine. Elle a cette particularité d'être annoncée dès la préface, qui conditionne de fait la réception du récit par le lecteur. L'auteur y développe un programme où s'accumulent les références classiques: mélange de l'utile et de l'amusant (salut à Horace), censure des vices et des ridicules (sur le modèle de la comédie), respect du vraisemblable, condamnation des «puérilités fastueuses» du grand roman, des Turcs et des souterrains (ceci vise Prévost, bien entendu), le naturel, les convenances, la raison, représenter «l'homme tel qu'il est», et se garder des «applications» (salut cette fois à Boileau et à ses propos sur la satire), on ne voit guère qui pourrait s'opposer à un projet si éminemment raisonnable, qui constitue un abrégé des lieux communs qui s'échangent sur le genre romanesque depuis 1660. Admirable sagesse, en vérité, de la part de l'auteur de *l'Ecumoire*, qui, pour mieux faire, dédie l'œuvre à son illustre père, Crébillon le tragique. Enfin à promettre qu'il ne s'agira que d'amour, l'écrivain semble nous garantir des bassesses où peuvent tomber des héros contraints de chercher fortune et sujets à rencontrer des cochers de fiacre ou des chevaliers de la manchette — et voilà qui répond à la demande de distinction.

L'intention morale prend au reste une forme démonstrative qu'elle n'avait ni chez Prévost ni chez Marivaux. Même si l'on prend au sérieux l'assimilation par Prévost de *Manon* à un «traité de morale», les deux romanciers se sont bien gardés de présenter le trajet de leurs personnages comme exemplaire[3]. Crébillon, lui, ne fait rien moins qu'imposer un protocole de lecture à son lecteur. Trois temps sont fixés:

    i.   «un homme tel qu'ils sont presque tous dans une extrême jeunesse, simple et sans art», premières amours;

ii.   le temps «des fausses idées», en clair le libertinage mondain; et

iii.   le retour à soi, grâce à «une femme estimable».

C'est dans ce troisième moment que le héros vieilli écrit ses mémoires, d'un lieu de retraite, ou du moins de retrait, familier aux mémorialistes. Ce beau programme, on le sait, sera interrompu au quinzième jour de l'histoire, qui trouve son dénouement dans la perte d'un pucelage. Crébillon a tenu parole, il ne s'est agi que d'amour. Ou peut-être, dirions-nous aujourd'hui, de sexualité.

La préface prépare donc l'entrée en scène du narrateur. Tout laisse penser que ce narrateur qu'on nous dit dégagé des «fausses idées», a accédé aux vraies. Cette posture d'homme ou de femme d'expérience, connue de Marivaux et de Prévost, semble garantir l'accès du narrateur à ce que l'auteur tient pour la vérité. Du fait de cette circulation du sens entre texte et paratexte, évitée par les deux autres romanciers, une certaine confusion peut se produire entre instances auctorielle et narratorielle.

Or c'est bien en sujet de savoir que se présente le narrateur de Crébillon. Le trait est rendu sensible par le fait que le jeune héros est aussitôt caractérisé comme le sujet d'un non-savoir, et copieusement tourné en ridicule par le narrateur, pour son innocence et sa naïveté, origines de bourdes et de faux-pas dont l'effet est le plus souvent comique. Il y a de l'enfant, du bon (?) sauvage et du Thomas Diafoirus dans cet ingénu du grand monde. Non sans frôler l'invraisemblable, l'auteur le condamne à une interprétation systématiquement déplacée de la réalité qui l'entoure[4]. On a donc affaire à un narrateur violemment critique qui ne cesse de se juger lui-même du haut de son savoir actuel et n'en finit pas de s'émerveiller des abîmes de son ignorance d'autrefois[5]. Pour reprendre les termes de Gérard Genette, le point de vue *actoriel* (celui du jeune Meilcour) est presque systématiquement celui du leurre, tandis que le *narratoriel* est supposé porteur de vérité. L'écart entre ces deux registres est attendu, mais il atteint ici une ampleur exceptionnelle, au point qu'un double récit pourrait parfois sembler nécessaire.

Nous avons affaire à une narration autodiégétique, en focalisation interne. Comme l'a rappelé Genette, la voix n'implique pas le point de vue. Il arrive à bien des écuyers ou suivantes du roman baroque, narrant l'aventure de leurs maîtres, d'oublier qu'ils ne pénètrent pas le secret des consciences. Mais dans le code du roman-mémoires de l'époque, l'usage de l'écriture à la première personne est pris au sérieux, ce qui implique certaines conséquences: le narrateur s'interdit de pénétrer directement la *psyché* des autres, sauf en cas d'émotions violentes produisant des signes non équivoques, quitte à compenser la restriction de champ par le biais des «sembla» et «parut», ou encore par une description psychologique qui se donne pour le fruit d'une reconstruction ultérieure. D'autre part, les énoncés généraux que produit le narrateur ne sauraient, pour le lecteur, posséder qu'une valeur relative: on ne peut les faire systématiquement endosser par l'auteur, car leur production est due aussi aux exigences de l'entreprise narrative[6]. Ce qui ne veut pas dire pour autant que ces énoncés manquent toujours de pertinence. La démarche adoptée par Crébillon, par la ressemblance qu'elle induit entre romancier et narrateur, tend plutôt à conforter la vérité générale des énoncés de ce dernier. Bref à nous rapprocher de la situation du récit non personnel où nous sommes portés à attribuer ces énoncés à l'auteur lui-même.

Un narrateur romancier ?

Le narrateur se transforme-t-il pour autant en romancier omniscient? Sans doute peut-on trouver que c'est infraction à la limitation de champ que d'affirmer que la mère du héros trouva, à se consacrer uniquement à son éducation son *plaisir* et «moins de difficultés que toute autre personne de son rang n'aurait fait» (69). Qu'en sait-il? Mais après tout les exigences d'un récit nécessairement sommaire, à cet endroit, peuvent justifier une présentation synthétique.

Pas d'infraction au code de la première personne, dans le passage qui suit, où Meilcour rend compte du «manque» qui lui survient («tout manquait à mon cœur» (70)). Une remarque cependant: il est au moins malaisé de distinguer, pour un certain nombre d'énoncés, ce qui relève du narratoriel et de l'actoriel. «Mon cœur»: est-ce le héros qui parle ou le narrateur désignant une demande sexuelle, en rapport avec l'âge, comme le marque le texte[7]. De même pour le «commerce des femmes», qui peut renvoyer à des réalités diverses. Entre corps et cœur, on peut hésiter[8]. On y reviendra.

Sous couvert de l'inexpérience du héros, le point de vue narratoriel prend franchement le dessus, avec le grand morceau sur «les femmes de mon temps». Le tableau qui est alors présenté est précisément celui que Meilcour n'a pas su voir, l'envers, en quelque sorte de sa vision. C'est pourtant sans infraction ouverte au régime du roman-mémoires. Le narrateur vieilli revêt les habits du moraliste (un amateur y est autorisé) et use du privilège de ce type de discours qui est de pouvoir représenter vraisemblablement une pensée collective. La Bruyère n'est pas loin. On reconnaîtra un antiféminisme familier au genre même, de nature à plaire à ceux qui ont apprécié le moralisme de la préface. Morceau brillant sans aucun doute, dont nous n'avons pas de raisons de mettre la vérité en question (sauf en ce qui touche un anachronisme volontaire et ironique, qui suppose la vertu des contemporaines, mais le clin d'œil est assez évident[9]). Cette veine moraliste alimente, on le sait, une bonne part du texte.

Une autre tradition autorise l'évocation en focalisation interne de Mme de Lursay, tout de suite après: le portrait est supposé être le fruit d'une familiarité avec le personnage, qui le rend aussi transparent aux yeux du narrateur qu'il était obscur à ceux du héros. On se souviendra du portrait de Mme de Miran par Marianne, encore que Marivaux ait pris soin de le placer assez longtemps après son entrée en scène (alors qu'ici le portrait précède l'action). Comme le faisait la préface à l'égard de l'histoire, la tirade moraliste et le portrait proposent en tous cas au lecteur une voie interprétative. On pourrait considérer dans ces occurrences que le narrateur effectue un passage à la limite de ses droits, que semble mettre en valeur une certaine impertinence de la diction, affichant sa qualité à la fois littéraire et mondaine. Bref c'est sans discrétion que s'exhibe notre sujet de savoir...

L'infraction est beaucoup plus nette dès qu'entre en action Mme de Lursay. «Elle m'avait pénétré» (73), déclare le narrateur. Et en retour, il la pénètre. Autrement dit: je ne savais pas, elle savait, et maintenant je sais, notamment ce qu'elle savait. Car c'est du point de vue de Mme de Lursay que l'action va être le plus souvent envisagée. Là encore nous supposons qu'il s'agit de reconstitution après coup, à quoi ont pu servir les confidences faites plus tard à Meilcour par sa maîtresse. Mais le narrateur tend à excéder ses droits coutumiers. Il lui arrive de se comporter en romancier omniscient, lorsqu'il débusque la pensée de derrière dissimulée par telle ou telle réplique: il est peu probable qu'après coup Mme de Lursay ait épluché leurs conversations passées à ce point de détail. Rarement le narrateur daigne consentir à une ignorance, traduite par des motivations multiples, entre lesquelles il laisse le lecteur choisir[10]. Parfois on se demande qui a bien pu voir ce qu'il raconte: «une joie douce éclatait dans ses yeux», déclare le narrateur qui, au même moment dit interpréter sourires et regards tendres comme autant d'insultes. Qui a bien pu être le récepteur de cette «joie douce»[11]? La rigueur d'écriture de Crébillon semble pourtant exclure l'hypothèse de la négligence.

Nul doute que le point de vue de Mme de Lursay ou celui du narrateur «éclairé» soit plus «intéressant» que celui d'un héros caractérisé par sa stupidité. Le comportement de l'ingénu crébillonien est d'une redoutable simplicité: aux prises avec le «manque», il a affaire à un «vouloir-aimer», qui s'appuie à la fois sur la demande pulsionnelle et l'exemple mondain, et qui trouve obstacle dans la terreur que lui inspirent le femmes[12]. Il n'a même pas droit à cette étape rituelle de la demande amoureuse, analysée par Claude Reichler, qu'est l'idéalisation: il n'idéalise pas, il a peur d'être humilié. Il ne s'agit pas de mettre en question l'intérêt et l'originalité de cette analyse qui approche de façon très neuve la question de la sexualité. Mais elle implique un appauvrissement du point de vue du héros. Son attention aux intérêts de son moi lui ferme proprement les yeux sur l'objet supposé de sa flamme: Mme de Lursay peut avoir des charmes (évoqués de façon convaincante), mais elle est choisie en raison de sa commodité et de sa proximité. La description psychologique du héros tend donc à se réduire à la répétition des symptômes de terreur et d'embarras, mécanique dont Crébillon tire d'excellents effets comiques[13]. Le narrateur est contraint de suppléer le héros pour ce qui est du rapport au réel. Tout autrement complexe apparaît le comportement d'une Lursay appliquée à faire sortir de sa stupidité ce jeune Arlequin pas encore poli par l'amour.

Ce début du roman s'inscrit dans la perspective interprétative suggérée par la préface: Mme de Lursay, fausse dévote habile, qui hérite de toute évidence de la Mme de Ferval de Marivaux dans le *Paysan parvenu*, est donnée comme une de ces femmes dont le narrateur a fait le portrait général. Sensuelle, mais rendue prudente par quelque mésaventure, elle fait montre d'une habileté que le narrateur surprend après coup:

> Quelques soupirs, qu'elle affectait de ne pousser qu'à demi, achevèrent de me confondre; [...] Madame de Lursay avait trop d'expérience pour se méprendre à son ouvrage, et n'en pas profiter. (113–14)

Le récit abonde en notations de cette espèce. Cette machiniste a même préparé le discours destiné à excuser sa chute (c'est le système «platonicien», dont se gaussera Versac, et que le narrateur traite de «discours rebattu»)[14]. Araignée tapie dans sa toile, attendant qu'à ses fils se prenne notre ingénu, cette femme à projets a déjà quelque chose de la future Mme de Merteuil:

> Elle avait étudié avec soin son sexe et le nôtre, et connaissait tous les ressorts qui les font agir. Patiente dans ses vengeances comme dans ses plaisirs, elle savait les attendre du temps, lorsque le moment ne les lui fournissait pas. (74)

Par définition, on ne saurait donc attendre d'elle qu'un discours et un comportement leurrants, dont le héros semble devoir être la victime.

D'où le paradoxe du discours final: Mme de Lursay, que le héros a cru surprendre avec un amant, confond son accusateur et raconte à nouveau l'histoire que nous venons de lire, mais cette fois de son point de vue. Le discours est émouvant et convaincant et répond à toutes les questions que le lecteur est en droit de se poser. Mme de Lursay y fait une superbe analyse de la «belle résistance» qu'a offert le jeune homme et de l'absurdité de ses présupposés: s'attendait-il à la trouver vierge? Et affirme la légitimité pour une femme de céder à sa passion, sans pour autant être traitée avec mépris. Ce discours est peut-être le comble de l'habileté, et qu'il réduise le héros au silence ne surprendra pas, vu la circonstance. Mais le narrateur qui le rapporte s'abstient d'en démonter la machine. Le sujet de savoir fait silence lui aussi, laissant le lecteur face à une vérité qu'il ne semble pas contester, réduit à trouver une preuve bien pauvre de machiavélisme dans la disposition d'un fauteuil[15]. Il ne retrouve qu'avec peine un peu de cette ironie dont il accablait volontiers cette «dame si délicate»[16]. Mais il ne met pas explicitement en question les suggestions antérieures. On n'en est pas moins à bonne distance du schéma que proposait le début du roman.

On laissera ici de côté la question de la genèse: Crébillon, séduit par son personnage, a pu être entraîné où il ne songeait pas, bref être plus sensible à Mme de Lursay qu'il ne le croyait. Nous importe en revanche le résultat textuel, tel qu'accepté par son auteur, qui maintient un écart entre le début et la fin, contraignant à questionner la validité et la cohérence du discours narratoriel, mais aussi à supposer que Crébillon a bien pu mettre en scène la *dérive* de ce discours, introduisant ainsi une *temporalité* dans le temps de l'énonciation, absente, me semble-t-il, chez Prévost et Marivaux. Ce à quoi nous fait assister Crébillon, n'est-ce pas la progressive défaillance du projet d'interprétation narratoriale, et donc à la défaite du sujet de savoir posé au début de l'œuvre? En d'autres termes, l'opération de remémoration et d'écriture semble bien modifier le narrateur, défaire ses certitudes initiales, sans qu'il consente à reconnaître sa défaite. Du même coup, on se demandera ce que vaut le savoir qu'il a étalé.

«Il s'en fallait beaucoup que je fusse d'accord avec moi-même»
Le narrateur moraliste parlait des femmes, collectif déjà abusif, en toute rigueur, puisqu'il ne s'agit, à moins d'absurdité que des femmes du monde. Il faut aussi exclure de cet ensemble les mères et les filles, puisque ni Hortense ni Mmes de Meilcour et de Théville ne répondent à la définition retenue. Restent donc Sénanges et Mongennes: il se trouve que l'une s'offre sans succès, et que l'autre renvoie Meilcour à une consommation ultérieure. Et Mme de Lursay. Avouons que pour la rapidité de la chute, elle n'est pas exemplaire. Vingt-quatre heures avaient suffi à Mme de Ferval pour se retrouver seule avec Jacob, à peine marié, dans une chambre fermée à clef[17]. Il est vrai que l'affaire entre Meilcour et Lursay se conclut en quinze jours, mais il a fallu deux longs mois pour qu'elle fasse le premier pas. C'est tout juste si le narrateur ne lui fait pas grief de sa maladresse, en évoquant leur «ridicule état»[18]. Effet de la prudence de la «femme à projets»? De fait, l'image initiale d'une intelligence supérieure mise au service de la sensualité se fissure vite. Le projet de se faire aimer sans être méprisée et de ménager la durée de la relation amoureuse appartient si peu au registre de l'amour mondain que le narrateur en vient, à propos de l'âge de Mme de Lursay, à élaborer une curieuse théorie selon laquelle il reviendrait à la femme vieillissante, moins sujette à l'amour-propre, d'être capable d'aimer vraiment. Il en

conclut que «ce qu'on croit la dernière fantaisie d'une femme, est bien souvent sa première passion»[19]. Le sentiment ne serait donc pas, pour Mme de Lursay, qu'un «sujet de conversation». L'effort pour dévaluer l'entreprise de la dame par la motivation (basse) de la peur est au moins maladroit, puisque cette peur appartient aussi au véritable «sentiment». Et que penser de l'application de ce principe à Hortense?

Le narrateur ne renonce jamais explicitement à l'idée de la femme «habile» qui entend le piéger. Mais à mesure qu'avance le roman, ses démonstrations sur ce point perdent de leur assurance et il avoue parfois ne pas tout s'expliquer de la conduite de sa partenaire. Le commentaire explicatif se fait de plus en plus discret tandis que le discours rapporté et le dialogue gagnent du terrain. Plus d'une fois, le discours narratoriel semble devenir discrètement le champ clos de deux interprétations — Lursay dissimulée, Lursay sensible — non sans qu'on frôle la contradiction. Il arrive au narrateur de se tirer de la difficulté en reconnaissant à Mme de Lursay une sensibilité dont elle ne serait pas consciente, énoncé difficile à accorder avec l'idée d'une sensibilité feinte, mais qui permet de préserver l'hypothèse de son machiavélisme[20].

A vrai dire, de son habileté et de sa lucidité, Mme de Lursay ne donne guère de preuves. Après la rencontre d'Hortense, elle est une dupe, en face du jeune homme qui calcule froidement les moyens de ménager celle qui est devenu pour lui un «second choix». Cette situation banale — la jeune surclasse son aînée —, elle l'avait prévue et exposée lors du premier aveu de Meilcour, mais quand elle devine la rivale, elle se trompe sur l'objet (Hortense et non Sénanges, comme elle le croit). Or, aux yeux de Meilcour, la rencontre avec l'inconnue suffit à justifier toutes les tromperies. Mme de Lursay prend clairement figure de victime, lorsque l'indifférence de son soupirant l'entraîne à se livrer aux reproches, puis à mendier un rendez-vous, auquel, avec une parfaite goujaterie, le héros ne se rendra que trop tard pour la voir seule. Meilcour reconnaît alors (avec une cruauté pour laquelle le narrateur n'a pas un mot de regret) sa propre maîtrise:

> et, voyant qu'elle ne me disait mot, j'allai m'amuser à regarder jouer: il n'y avait assurément rien de moins honnête que mon procédé; aussi me parut-il la

fâcher vivement; mais il m'importait peu qu'elle s'en offensât, pourvu que je
ne la misse point à portée de me le dire. (113)

Qui ici manœuvre l'autre? A ce stade cependant, Meilcour n'a rien à reprocher
à Mme de Lursay. Au prix de l'humiliation, elle le ramène cependant à elle,
mais, le soir même, le fiasco comique de son partenaire terrorisé laisse au moins
supposer qu'il est quelques «ressorts» de l'éveil sexuel qui lui échappent. La fin
de la soirée montre en tous cas que l'image d'une Lursay sinon impudique, du
moins déterminée, suggérée antérieurement, n'est guère soutenable.

Victime, Mme de Lursay l'est plus encore par la suite. Devenue, grâce aux
ragots de Versac, objet de haine pour Meilcour, elle subit de sa part une entreprise violente dont Meilcour ne dissimule pas l'extrême grossièreté[21]. Le même
jour, Versac la ridiculise aux yeux de son soupirant en exhibant l'odieux guignol
qu'est Pranzi. A demi violée le matin, insultée par les deux hommes l'après-
midi, Mme de Lursay finit la journée en se trouvant une rivale en Mme de
Sénanges. Elle ne rencontrera aucune pitié le lendemain chez Meilcour, qui
l'accable de sa froideur et du «jargon d'usage» et déclare sa satisfaction: «L'état
où je la mettais flattait cependant ma vanité; c'était un spectacle nouveau pour
moi, mais qui m'amusait sans m'attendrir[...][22]». Compte rendu clinique où le
remords et le regret n'ont aucune part, où toute pitié est absente. L'absence de
ces affects attendus dessine aussi le portrait du narrateur, prompt à critiquer son
inexpérience, mais curieusement discret quant à l'évaluation morale de sa conduite[23]. Lursay prend pourtant des risques en recourant au moyen dangereux du
billet (qui ne lui vaudra du reste qu'un refus supplémentaire), tout en ignorant
que sa démarche facilitait les rencontres de Meilcour avec sa rivale... Le tout
sans que ses mésaventures compromettent sa dignité.

Au cours du récit, l'image initiale de l'*habile* s'est bel et bien effondrée,
sans que le narrateur en prenne acte. Tout entier occupé à défendre sa belle
passion et à ne pas perdre la face, le narrateur ne semble regretter de ses exploits
passés que le ridicule qu'ils ont pu lui donner. Dans la scène finale, il fournira
l'image d'une Lursay indéniablement émouvante, sans paraître prendre conscience de la difficulté à intégrer cette image dans l'ensemble de son discours. Par
cette curieuse procédure, le romancier conduit son lecteur à éprouver des affects

dont le narrateur est incapable, ou du moins dont il est incapable de saisir la portée, et donc à s'écarter de la position d'identification avec ce narrateur, qui lui était d'abord proposée. C'est dire que le point de vue du narrateur, supposé omniscient au début, révèle une singulière étroitesse — de cœur et d'esprit, serait-on tenté de dire.

On appréciera la subtilité avec laquelle Crébillon manie l'à peu près: «Coquette jadis et même un peu galante», dit d'abord le narrateur de Mme de Lursay. Le portrait initial n'est pas franchement faux. L'héroïne y a bien la quarantaine que lui conteste Versac (qui d'ailleurs avoue plus tard la calomnie). L'expression est floue, un peu faible pour les trois amants durant le mariage, et cinq ou six après que lui attribue Versac. Mais déclarer aussitôt après: «Malgré l'air prude qu'elle avait pris, on s'obstinait toujours à la soupçonner; et j'étais peut-être le seul à qui elle en eût imposé.» (73), c'est laisser penser le pire, et rendre vraisemblable la dizaine d'amants que lui attribue Versac. Mais est-ce cohérent avec l'intime amitié que professent à son égard Mmes de Meilcour et de Théville, vertueuses de profession[24]? Mme de Lursay a-t-elle à se reprocher autre chose que le regrettable Pranzi? Cela paraît au moins probable, encore que la dame reste sur ce point, dans son discours final, fort discrète. Mais à ce moment, la question n'est plus là.

Mme de Lursay est donc de moins en moins l'échantillon représentatif des femmes dont le narrateur brossait le portrait. De fait, ses attributs «dévaluants» semblent se répartir, dès la seconde partie, sur deux autres personnages: la sensualité impudique sur la «coquette délabrée» qu'est Mme de Sénanges, le machiavélisme calculateur sur Mme de Mongennes, toutes deux dépourvues de grâces et soucieuses de la parade mondaine[25]. En cours de route, au reste Lursay change de rôle: s'il lui était attribué de vouloir faire l'éducation (mondaine, s'entend) de Meilcour, c'est à Sénanges que revient en définitive la charge de le faire entrer dans le monde et de l'empoisonner de son mauvais savoir[26]. Dans la scène finale, c'est bien une Lursay timide, inquiète, amoureuse qui prononce la phrase étonnante où se marque la prédominance du rapport personnel: «je suis perdue si je ne suis pas heureuse» (245). Jamais le romancier et le narrateur n'ont présenté une figure aussi *aimable* de Mme de Lursay qu'en cet instant où le héros croit découvrir qu'il ne l'aime pas.

Le narrateur aveugle

«Quelque enchanté que je fusse, mes yeux s'ouvrirent enfin.» Le vide dans l'âme
prélude au retour de l'image d'Hortense et à des remords dont le héros ressent
lui-même l'absurdité[27]. Le personnage d'Hortense mérite qu'on s'y arrête, car le
point de vue du narrateur à son égard présente, sinon une anomalie, du moins
des caractères propres à décevoir l'attente du lecteur, de manière peut-être parallèle à ce qui se passe pour Lursay, par un usage conscient de la technique du
narrateur aveugle.

La rencontre de Meilcour et de la belle inconnue, à l'Opéra, obéit, on le
sait, si bien aux canons romanesques que Meilcour le remarque lui-même, y
voyant la marque des «grandes aventures». On aura un écho plaisant de ce
romanesque lors de la seconde rencontre aux Tuileries, où Meilcour paralysé par
sa timidité rêve d'une entorse providentielle qui l'autoriserait à parler à sa belle
— entorse qui vient évidemment de *La Vie de Marianne*[28]. De façon marquée —
trop marquée, peut-être — Hortense vient occuper la place de l'objet d'amour,
entendons du grand amour, du vrai amour qui va de pair avec la vertu. Une
anti-Lursay en quelque sorte, qui a suscité une passion portant les signes topi-
ques: soudaineté, violence, réciprocité, perfection de l'objet. Sa place pourrait
être celle de la femme «estimable» annoncée dans la préface, encore que le terme
soit déplacé par rapport au personnage qui nous est présenté. La timidité du
héros et l'intensité de ses sentiments peuvent expliquer qu'il ne prenne pas
conscience de l'intérêt que lui manifeste la jeune fille, encore qu'il lui faille
beaucoup d'ingéniosité pour parvenir à ignorer que l'inconnu évoqué aux
Tuileries ne peut guère être que lui (la candidature de Germeuil étant écartée par
des indices assez clairs)[29]. Pour le lecteur, le romancier a voulu que les choses
soient claires: l'intérêt marqué à l'Opéra, la confession des Tuileries, sous forme
dénégative, la distraction et la rêverie sombre chez Mme de Lursay, l'attention
au malaise du héros, la conversation sur l'inconstance, tout cela ne laisse aucun
doute: Hortense commence à aimer le héros, en est troublée, et aussi peu expéri-
mentée que lui, se comporte exactement de la même manière. S'il détourne le
regard, elle baisse les yeux[30]. De l'inexpérience relèvent les déclarations pré-
somptueuses contre les amants aussi bien que les méditations sur l'inconstance.

C'est bien parce que Meilcour et Hortense se ressemblent qu'ils ne parviennent pas à s'entendre.

Or ici, de façon inattendue, le point de vue actoriel triomphe. Ce que le lecteur perçoit par dessus son épaule, le narrateur semble condamné à l'ignorer, frappé d'un soudain aveuglement de sa capacité interprétative. Il partage l'ignorance du héros. Trait plus étrange: même si l'on peut souhaiter qu'Hortense soit la femme «estimable», rien ne vient assurer d'un avenir. Pas la moindre de ces prolepses dont le narrateur use volontiers pour disserter à son aise des autres personnages. A admettre qu'Hortense soit un objet perdu, on attendrait du moins que le narrateur, avec son expérience, fût capable d'interpréter la conduite de la jeune fille. Or point. Le romancier ayant déjà abattu ses cartes, on ne peut guère d'autre part invoquer un arbitraire de la régie narrative, qui soustrairait au lecteur une vérité cependant perçue. Rien ne permet donc d'affirmer que, selon l'exemple des grands romans, Meilcour ait retrouvé Hortense, ni même qu'il ait fait l'expérience heureuse de l'amour vrai. Si l'aveuglement du narrateur persiste, c'est peut-être que cet amour-là n'a jamais existé que dans l'imaginaire. Ce qui se paierait de l'incapacité à rien savoir de l'autre.

La scène finale conduit, on le sait, après l'extase, («mes yeux s'ouvrirent enfin») à un retour au clivage traditionnel: illusion des sens v. amour véritable (autrement dit, dans le langage du narrateur: *sentiment*[31]). Ainsi se trouverait démontrée la supériorité de l'un sur l'autre, et accessoirement les avantages de la vertu. Ce triomphe de l'amour serait plus convaincant sans doute s'il se référait à une expérience *effective* de bonheur, si l'on pouvait réduire le rapport à Lursay à une pure jouissance physique, si aussi le héros n'avouait pas qu'il compte bien la retrouver le lendemain... Bref est-ce de manière tout à fait creuse que Mme de Lursay emploie le terme de *sentiment*? Le narrateur y insiste: le bonheur qu'il obtient avec elle relève de l'*erreur*. Et de s'appliquer à une ironie bien dérisoire sur son respect des bienséances, non sans reconnaître pourtant: «il s'en fallait beaucoup que je fusse d'accord avec moi-même» (248). Ce désaccord n'est-il pas toujours présent? Quel *enchantement* a ici opéré, se demande Meilcour, tel un autre Tanzaï. Mais Mme de Lursay n'est pas la fée Concombre[32]. Et Meilcour admet qu'elle *mérite* le plaisir qu'il lui donne pour calmer ses inquiétudes: moment essentiel où, pour la première fois, Meilcour traite sa partenaire comme sujet à part entière et parvient enfin, à ce moment, sur un mode inattendu, à la respecter[33]. De toute évidence, le clivage évoqué plus haut reste bien pauvre pour interpréter la réalité évoquée.

«Sans connaître ce qui me manquait, je sentis du vide dans mon âme» (246). La parenté de la formule avec celle qui est employée au début du récit, au temps de «l'ennui intérieur», amène une question: est-ce que plus encore qu'à un banal *post coitum animal triste*, cette phrase ne renvoie pas au destin qui serait celui de toute relation amoureuse *réelle*? Le retour de l'image d'Hortense ne serait alors qu'un recours à l'imaginaire pour compenser un échec inévitable, pour remplir d'un espoir le manque qui fait retour. Nul doute qu'une fois amorcée l'expérience amoureuse, Meilcour, libéré de l'angoisse de la première fois, a cru reconnaître en Hortense celle qui détenait le remède au manque. Il l'imagine du moins. Qu'en serait-il à l'épreuve? On n'en sait rien. En tant que figure imaginaire, Hortense présente tous les avantages: elle réactive le désir d'être le premier et le seul, dont Mme de Lursay a montré la vanité, elle sauve Meilcour de l'emprise exclusive (et donc dangereuse pour le moi) de la femme qui le domine, et peut-être aussi des relents vaguement incestueux que comporte une relation *intime* avec l'amie *intime* de sa mère (et cela pourrait rendre compte de la culpabilité irraisonnée évoquée plus haut)[34]. Le dernier avantage n'est-il pas dans cette inaccessibilité même, qui autorise le héros de se rendre à nouveau coupable, bref de continuer à vivre, comme le constate Meilcour avec une curieuse désinvolture[35]? A rester dans l'imaginaire, Hortense n'a-t-elle pas rempli tout son rôle? Le double jeu de l'auteur autorise les bonnes âmes à rêver un triomphe vertueux de l'amour. En attendant, la seule véritable relation d'échange a bien lieu avec Mme de Lursay, permettant l'accès à une altérité qui fait que Meilcour, même sans amour (du moins le croit-il), se sent le devoir d'apaiser les inquiétudes que son indifférence peut faire naître chez elle et que, dit-il, elle «ne méritait pas». Amour ou pas, on échappe ici à l'univers de l'agression et de la peur, pour entrer dans celui du don en retour. N'est-ce pas celui aussi de la civilisation, à ne pas confondre, même si elle en a besoin, avec les bienséances en usage? Il y a donc bien une éducation, même si ce n'est pas celle qui sert à entrer dans le «monde» (ce grand monde qui n'est pas l'univers). Or le narrateur ne semble pas percevoir la portée d'une expérience qu'il ne sait qu'encadrer dans le schéma binaire illusion des sens/sentiment.

N'est-ce pas indiquer l'insuffisance de ce schéma lui-même, que le vécu excède? Les divers aveuglements et défaillances du narrateur ne sont-ils pas dus au conformisme même de son interprétation? Cette hypothèse conduit à interroger l'intention qui peut sous-tendre une si curieuse stratégie. A supposer une infirmité interprétative qui ne frapperait pas de nullité tout le discours du moraliste, mais qui lui conférerait une valeur relative, à déterminer dans chaque cas par le lecteur (et n'est-ce pas une des leçons du livre que ce nécessaire flottement de la signification?), l'affichage initial du narrateur comme sujet de savoir fait partie d'un leurre qu'il appartient au lecteur de découvrir[36]. De ce leurre, on est bien obligé de conclure que le préfacier est complice en nous assurant du savoir du narrateur. On s'expliquerait mieux dès lors le caractère *un peu trop* conformiste de cette préface, comme l'imitation un peu trop voyante des moralistes classiques. Mais familier des passages à la limite, Crébillon s'y prend avec assez de discrétion pour que le lecteur ait le choix de l'interprétation et puisse se satisfaire éventuellement de l'opposition traditionnelle sens/sentiment, tout en maintenant sa croyance en l'idéale union de l'amour et de la vertu. Il n'en fallait peut-être pas moins pour faire accepter une œuvre qui abordait pour la première fois (car les héros de Marivaux et de Prévost ont d'autres soucis) la question infiniment délicate de l'entrée dans la sexualité. Rien ne pouvait mieux se prêter à cette entreprise que le langage à la fois décent et obscène d'un mondain devenu moraliste qui garderait quelque peu les œillères tout à la fois de la mondanité, de la passion et de la vertu. Faut-il alors discerner un demi-aveu dans la première phrase de la Préface: «Les Préfaces, pour la plus grande partie, ne semblent faites que pour en imposer au Lecteur» (65).

Crébillon n'attaque pas de front le mythe de la grande passion, il se contente de le situer dans l'imaginaire (même s'il montre comment la posture de la passion s'accommode fort bien de complaisances narcissiques[37]). Il ne s'en prend pas non plus à la vertu, même si ses vertueuses sont étrangement froides[38]. Il ne critique pas le discours moraliste de savoir, mais exhibe ses défaillances, et surtout désigne le modèle d'un autre discours, éminemment féminin, qui ne cacherait pas son rapport au désir, et présenterait l'avantage de faire avancer vers le bonheur: celui de Mme de Lursay.

Cette hypothèse, le discours de Versac à l'Etoile me semble la confirmer. Le petit-maître a raison de voir en Mme de Lursay son principal adversaire. Car il est le représentant par excellence du discours de savoir, lui qui prétend communiquer au jeune homme qui l'admire, cette «science du monde», à laquelle un piètre jeu de mots donne couleur philosophique. Faut-il s'y laisser prendre et envisager le personnage à travers les lunettes en somme idéalisantes de Laclos? Le cours magistral à sa propre gloire, que le petit maître administre au néophyte, est souvent traité avec indulgence par la critique, malgré (ou à cause de?) son incroyable pédantisme. Il est vrai que Versac y met à contribution les théoriciens de la civilité et les moralistes classiques, leur pessimisme et leur antiféminisme. Mais ces références perverties ne servent qu'un idéal parfaitement contraire à celui de la civilité: étayer le triomphe d'un moi solitaire, tout entier requis par la quête du pouvoir et d'une gloire que prive de sens l'absence de référence à un sujet collectif (Versac ne se reconnaît d'autre juge que lui-même, et il hérite en ce sens du Clitandre de Corneille dans *La Place Royale*). Certes le programme qu'il déroule n'a rien d'une partie de plaisir (et le jeune homme, qui lui prête une attention distraite, estime tout bonnement que le jeu n'en vaut pas la chandelle). C'est en quoi il peut séduire le lecteur moral. Mais pour la défense d'un *moi* si précieux que Versac n'ose jamais le montrer, ce programme suppose que le sujet se masque jusqu'à se défigurer lui-même. Il ne peut se faire «reconnaître» qu'à force d'être méconnu. Quant à son pouvoir supposé, il ne peut se maintenir que dans un système de relations dont pourtant Versac dénonce l'absurdité. Choix peu satisfaisant, d'après le narrateur, puisque Versac, héritier à cet égard des libertins impuissants du *Sopha*, n'en imagine pas moins, selon le narrateur, l'amour dont il est incapable[39]. A la base, un motif peu héroïque: la peur devant les femmes, étrangement proche de celle de Meilcour, qui du moins a encore le bon sens de ne pas vouloir séduire celles qu'il ne désire pas. Là dessus, Meilcour pose une question évidemment fondamentale: «pourquoi avons-nous besoin qu'une femme nous mette dans le monde?» (222). Or le Mentor se dérobe, craignant d'aller «trop loin» et réclamant l'espace d'un autre cours. Quant à ses exploits, ils ne sont guère éclatants: à l'égard d'Hortense, il manifeste un étrange aveuglement et une fort sotte confiance aux vertus de sa belle jambe. La manière dont il calomnie et ridiculise Mme de Lursay est une bien maigre preuve de ses prétentions à la monarchie de l'univers mondain[40]. Ce rêve d'empire universel apparaît bien comme une des solutions possibles à l'incertitude connue par le jeune Meilcour à ses débuts: à défaut d'une, choisir toutes les femmes pour n'en rien perdre et ne pas perdre son image de soi[41]. Loin de dissiper les craintes que peut garder Meilcour à l'endroit des femmes, ce discours ne peut que les aggraver. D'ailleurs de quoi rêve Versac ? d'être celui qui met dans le monde les femmes qui mettent les hommes dans le monde — la femme des femmes en quelque sorte, ou leur mère, comme y invite l'expression[42]. Malgré la référence insistante aux moralistes, il conviendrait de ne pas négliger ce que ce discours a d'incohérent et de délirant, quitte à se demander si la caution que Versac cherche chez eux n'en est pas, pour Crébillon, une critique indirecte[43]. Versac semble prendre, à l'Etoile, le rôle du père qui a manqué à Meilcour: son discours de savoir se révèle défaillant et inefficace sur un auditeur pourtant d'avance séduit. La parole féminine de Mme de Lursay (qui lui succède) aura un tout autre pouvoir et une tout autre vérité.

Ce point de vue sur Versac importe à notre analyse du discours du narrateur. Successeur et vainqueur de son Mentor, Meilcour a renoncé aux prestiges de cette fausse philosophie. Il n'en appartient pas moins à un très grand monde, pour lequel Crébillon n'a jamais marqué de sympathie et qui tend à confondre l'univers mondain avec l'univers tout court. Sans frapper de nullité sa parole, cette appartenance n'en marque-t-elle pas les limites? Cela conduirait à interroger un *à peu près* de la préface: est-il sûr que ce fils de très grande famille qui n'a certes pas les soucis de carrière de des Grieux et est assuré de lendemains confortables, soit le représentant de tous les jeunes gens de son âge? Encore une fois on a affaire à une généralisation hâtive, mais commode pour soutenir la moralité de l'entreprise. De fait, le libertin en action et le libertin devenu moraliste ont ceci de commun qu'ils manifestent un penchant affirmé pour l'exercice de la pulsion de savoir, qui se déploie, dans les deux cas, contre les femmes et en particulier contre Mme de Lursay. On pourrait considérer que la manière dont le narrateur semble vouloir d'abord régler son compte à cette dernière, est un dernier effort pour la maîtriser, par les moyens de l'intelligence, à travers l'écriture — en somme la dernière manifestation de la *belle résistance* qu'il lui a opposée, et qu'il oppose encore à son souvenir. La dynamique des *Egarements* tient aussi à ce qu'on y suit l'histoire d'un discours et d'un projet qui échappe aux intentions de son narrateur — le récit d'une énonciation. Curieusement l'intention moralisatrice et explicative ne serait pas si loin de celle du libertin, dans cette commune perspective de maîtrise. C'est bien parce que le vécu excède cette maîtrise que nous avons droit à Mme de Lursay et à cette relation unique que le romancier renonce à nommer dans le cadre de l'opposition amour vertueux/libertinage. Que Versac, à cet endroit du roman, occupe la place du père attendu et dont le narrateur a été privé par sa mort, c'est bien évident. Qu'il soit défaillant dans cet office, ne l'est pas moins, même si l'on annonce son triomphe prochain. C'est auprès de Mme de Lursay que Meilcour apprend à vivre. Faut-il admettre que c'est à la fin de son récit que le narrateur comprend qu'il l'aimait, ou qu'il regrette de n'avoir pas su l'aimer? Ce serait glisser vers un fantasme que Crébillon n'a pas totalement découragé. Est-ce l'auteur des *Lettres de la Marquise* qui prend sa revanche?

Appendice épiloguant

Tout cela suppose un auteur masqué, s'amusant à prendre ses lecteurs au piège de la morale, pour mieux faire triompher les inavouables séductions du récit. Démarche dont on peut penser qu'elle a pu être consciente, quitte à la taxer de perverse.

Ce qui suit, inspiré par une problématique (à peu près) freudienne, a un rapport étroit avec ce qui précède. Mais on ne saurait sans abus en imputer la théorie à Crébillon. Ce que son texte donne à penser implique seulement la possibilité qu'il l'ait pensé.

On aura été sensible à la manière dont Meilcour souligne que l'apparition du *manque* est antérieure à l'apparition de l'*objet*, dont la commodité est essentielle et la nature relativement secondaire. Il se trouve que ce manque se manifeste au moment où le sujet doit s'écarter de la sphère familiale, où la mort du père l'a mis en tête à tête avec sa mère. Malgré la déclaration du narrateur, la relation avec la mère n'est pas marquée par une tendresse particulière, plutôt par une dépendance due à l'absence de relations avec le monde extérieur. On peut donc se demander si ne se trouve pas évoquée, de façon symbolique (et non psychologique) la relation duelle entre mère et enfant originée dans le rapport au ventre maternel, vouée à une série de ruptures qui se font écho les unes aux autres et dont la plus voyante est l'entrée dans la vie sexuelle. C'est bien de s'intéresser à ce moment (fait nouveau pour l'individu masculin, ce qui se traduit dans les *Egarements* en partie par une inversion des rôles sexuels, Meilcour racontant comment on l'a séduit) qui entraîne à se demander ce qui se passait avant[44]. Dans cette perspective, Freud supposait une horreur initiale pour l'objet qui est liée à la manière dont il contribue à troubler l'équilibre narcissique initial. Sans prendre en compte les divergences entre les auteurs, on peut admettre que ce manque se trouve en quelque sorte doué d'un statut par l'acceptation intériorisée de l'interdiction œdipienne. Cet écart entre le manque et l'objet est sans doute le trait le plus original de Crébillon par rapport à ses prédécesseurs, qui montre que ce n'est que dans un second temps (celui d'Hortense) que le choix de l'objet devient essentiel. L'insistance avec laquelle Crébillon a employé l'expression «mettre dans le monde», évocatrice d'un *mettre au monde*, laisse penser qu'il n'a pas tout ignoré de ce rapport à la mère que cherche Meilcour en Mme de Lursay (et dont le *Paysan parvenu* offrait évidemment une illustration). Il a souligné d'autre part tout ce que la demande de Meilcour comportait de narcissique. Meilcour se comporte avec toutes les femmes comme si elles étaient sa mère: le rapport sexuel est envisagé comme une insupportable agression. On comprend ce que dans ces circonstances peut porter l'exigence d'être *le premier* et *le seul*: elle est celle de l'enfant auprès de la mère. Mme de Lursay le fait accéder à l'âge adulte en lui permettant de supporter sa culpabilité, et en le faisant renoncer à une demande archaïque et totalitaire, qui aussi bien est demande d'éternité. La passion pourrait apparaître alors comme la résurgence de cette demande archaïque, qu'aucune relation *réelle* n'est susceptible de satisfaire. On voit comment elle est déterminée aussi par la nature de l'objet, la valeur qui lui est reconnue par les autres (succès de Hortense à l'Opéra), et le hasard des références littéraires (le roman...). Bref son rapport à la nature (que suppose le mythe de la passion) est au moins problématique. Elle pourrait être entendue comme une attitude régressive. On pourrait en dire autant du libertinage tel que l'entend Versac, qui en somme ne parvient pas à reconnaître l'existence de l'autre sexe et élabore une défense mégalomaniaque, où ne peut triompher que la pulsion agressive. L'attitude de Versac apparaît alors, avec le fétichisme des bienséances et des usages, comme une caricature de l'accès au symbolique que ménage Mme de Lursay à Meilcour, même s'il induit un passage par une position que l'on pourrait appeler dépressive (le sujet consent à sa propre modification), mais qui, à vrai dire, se nuance d'humour.

Une erreur, dit le narrateur. Peut-être. Le bonheur est peut-être à ce prix: celui de l'ignorance. Vais-je ajouter que les non-dupes errent? Ce ne serait pas si déplacé peut-être à propos d'un texte où les pères (ou les candidats à la fonction) marqués par l'éclat et le tumulte (du bruit en somme, et non de la parole) font si piètre figure face au radieux avatar de la mère, que perdit Crébillon, à l'âge de quatre ans[45].

UNIVERSITÉ DE PARIS III — SORBONNE NOUVELLE

NOTES

1. Gilot (Michel), «Les doux aveux de Crébillon», *Les paradoxes du romancier. Les «Égarements» de Crébillon*, sous la direction de Pierre Rétat, Presses Universitaires de Grenoble, 1975. Les numéros de pages sans autre mention dans la présente étude renvoient au texte des *Égarements* dans l'édition de Jean Dagen, GF, 1985.

2. En simplifiant, on dira que chez Marivaux le narrateur se fait plus ou moins complice de cette lecture critique, du moins jusqu'à un certain point, tandis que chez Prévost le narrateur, porté à la confession de ses fautes, semble ignorer les plus graves. Je renvoie sur ce point à la quatrième partie de mon *Roman à la première personne*, Colin, 1975.

3. Prévost plaide pour l'utilité de l'exercice identificatoire, et Marivaux se tient à distance de ses héros en se présentant comme «éditeur».

4. Le jeune Meilcour semble curieusement dépourvu de toute relation masculine et en est réduit à envisager de questionner sa mère sur la manière d'aborder les femmes... Ce fils de grande famille peut-il être à ce point coupé du monde social?

5. Posture clairement opposée à celle des narrateurs de Marivaux qui se complaisent à montrer comment le héros, malgré son inexpérience, possédait déjà un savoir qu'il ne pouvait formuler.

6.   Voir sur cette question chez Crébillon Carole Dornier, *Le Discours de maîtrise du libertin. Étude sur l'œuvre de Crébillon fils*, Klincksieck, 1994. En général pour le roman du XVIIIe siècle, mon étude «L'écrivain et son double dans le texte classique» in *Les sujets de l'écriture*, PUL, Lille 1981. La lecture romantique et même moderne des textes de Marivaux et Prévost (induite par la supposée «sincérité» de l'autobiographie) a négligé souvent cette incertitude pourtant essentielle au genre des mémoires et du coup a parfois abusivement confondu la vérité du narrateur et celle de l'auteur.

7.

     l'âge augmentant cette disposition à la tendresse, et me rendant leurs agréments plus sensibles. (70)

8.   Autrement dit on ne sait à quel point le jeune homme a pris conscience du caractère sexuel de sa demande, mais non plus quel crédit le narrateur fait à la distinction entre corps et cœur.

9.   Voir p. 72: «Les mœurs ont depuis ce temps-là si prodigieusement changé[...]» que le narrateur craint que le portrait des femmes «de son temps» (dont le libertinage succède à une vertu antique située dans un temps peu déterminé) ne paraisse invraisemblable. Cette disposition ternaire est parallèle à celle qui dans la préface articule la carrière du héros. Mais le factice du troisième temps est ici évident. Et donc...

10.   Voir par exemple p. 135–36:

     Je comptais, et avec quelque raison, ce me semble, que Madame de Lursay serait seule; mais, soit que ma façon de me comporter dans les rendez-vous lui eût déplu, soit qu'elle eût voulu me les faire désirer, elle avait décidé que je serais en proie à tous les importuns que mon destin pourrait amener chez elle ce jour-là.

11.   p. 83.

12.   Voir p. 70, «je voulais aimer, mais je n'aimais point».

13.   Cette mécanique signale la maladresse du héros, mais elle peut ne rien devoir à sa maladresse; ainsi lors de la quête d'Hortense, au nom de quoi Meilcour se refuse à voir Lursay, puis à accepter une sienne invitation: or Hortense est justement chez Lursay, et plus tard elle est de la partie de campagne rejetée.

14.   Voir p. 75 («sorte de discours rebattu, que tiennent sans cesse les trois quarts des femmes, et qui ne rend que plus méprisables celles qui le déshonorent par leur conduite») et p. 95.

15.
> Mon embarras augmenta encore quand elle m'ordonna (sans raison apparente
> à ce que je crus) de m'asseoir sur un fauteuil qui touchait à son canapé, ce qui
> me menait beaucoup plus près d'elle que je n'étais d'abord. (239)

16. Voir par exemple,

> Cette Dame si délicate, contente cependant de la façon dont je pensais sur son
> compte, jugea qu'il était temps de me donner de l'espérance, et de me faire
> penser, mais par les agaceries les plus décentes, que j'étais le mortel fortuné
> que son cœur avait choisi.

Meilcour se donne clairement pour dupe à ce moment. L'écho est à la fin plus ambigu:

> Grâces aux bienséances que Madame de Lursay observait sévèrement, elle me
> renvoya enfin [...]. (248)

17. Occasion de remarquer que les résistances apparentes de Mme de Ferval et de Mme de
Lursay ont des motifs fort différents. Et que s'affirmait déjà chez Marivaux l'opposition entre fausse dévote et libertin.

18.
> Il y avait au moins deux mois que nous étions dans ce ridicule état, lorsque
> Madame de Lursay, impatientée de son tourment, et de la vénération profonde que j'avais pour elle, résolut de se délivrer de l'un, en me guérissant de
> l'autre. (76)

19. p. 86.

20.
> Pendant toute la partie, Madame de Lursay, plus sensible qu'elle ne le croyait
> sans doute, emportée par son amour, m'en donna toutes les marques les plus
> fortes. (88)

Le narrateur n'en reconnaît pas moins que cette conduite répondait au besoin
qu'avait le héros d'être «rassuré».

21. Voir p. 140. Le narrateur se contente d'incriminer le désir de «décence» de Mme de
Lursay et sa propre inexpérience.

22. p. 172. Meilcour se croit autorisé à toutes les violences par la mauvaise opinion «sans
bornes» qu'il a prise de Lursay.

23. On se souviendra du rôle cardinal joué par la pitié, d'origine supposée naturelle ou providentielle, dans l'anthropologie du XVIIIe siècle.

24. Mme de Meilcour prend ouvertement sa défense contre Versac, tandis que Mme de Théville affaiblit sa défense en plaidant l'indifférence à la rumeur.

25. Dans la perspective génétique, un tournant serait donc pris en 1738, avec la seconde partie qui introduit Sénanges.

26. Voir p. 72–73

> si une des Dames, qui m'avait le plus vivement frappé, n'eût bien voulu se charger de mon éducation. La Marquise de Lursay (c'était son nom) me voyait presque tous les jours, ou chez elle, ou chez ma mère.

et p. 145

> Madame de Senanges à qui, comme on le verra dans la suite, j'ai eu le malheur de devoir mon éducation, était une de ces femmes philosophes [...].

27.

> Je l'avouerai même à ma honte, quelquefois je me justifiais mon procédé, et je ne concevais point comment j'avais pu manquer à Hortense, puisqu'elle ne m'aimait pas, que je ne lui avais rien promis, et que je ne pouvais pas espérer de lui devoir jamais autant de reconnaissance que j'en devais à Madame de Lursay. (248)

Le raisonnement n'est pas absurde, mais il est traité comme erreur par le narrateur.

28. Cette allusion révèle une lecture singulièrement pénétrante du texte de Marivaux: en se jetant sous son carrosse, Marianne abolit provisoirement l'espace qui la sépare de Valville, l'acte manqué permettant de réaliser le désir profond.

29. Le long monologue intérieur, après la seconde rencontre, fait arriver à une conclusion que laissait attendre les tergiversations antérieures: «Quand ce ne sera pas Germeuil, en serai-je moins malheureux?» (110).

30. Voir p. 110–11.

31. «ou que, dans l'ivresse où j'étais encore, le sentiment n'agît que faiblement sur moi» (248), dit par exemple le narrateur pour expliquer que le souvenir d'Hortense ne l'empêche pas de céder à nouveau aux charmes de Lursay.

32. On sait que dans *l'Ecumoire*, le prince Tanzaï ne peut retrouver sa virilité qu'en passant dans les bras de la fée monstrueuse. Peut-être faudrait-il penser à l'expérience parallèle de Néadarné dont les rapports forcés avec le génie Jonquille ne sont pas absolument de l'ordre du supplice.

33.

mais, malheureusement pour ma raison, elle s'aperçut que je rêvais, et m'en
montra une sorte d'inquiétude qu'il n'aurait pas été honnête de lui laisser, et
qu'en effet elle ne méritait pas d'avoir. Je la rassurai donc. (246)

Que la reconnaissance de l'autre s'opère sur ce mode, en dit long sur le refus de
Crébillon de réduire au physique le rapport libidinal.

34.   Retenons la curieuse formule de la page 73: «elle était de toutes les femmes celle que je
voyais le plus». Sans doute. Sur ce point, le *Paysan parvenu* ouvrait la voie.

35.   On pourrait interpréter la maladresse de Meilcour et son entêtement à se croire un
rival comme autant de tentatives pour ne pas approcher Hortense et la maintenir
dans l'imaginaire. Dans cette perspective, la manière dont, pour trouver Hortense, il
fuit Lursay chez qui se trouve Hortense, appartient clairement au registre de l'acte
manqué.

36.   Versac dénonce le creux, le non sens du langage mondain. Voir sur ce point l'étude de
Berthier (Philippe), «Le souper impossible». Telle n'est pas la position de Crébillon
qui, critiquant la croyance naïve de Meilcour, montre plutôt qu'un sens passe à
travers un usage conventionnel, mais qu'il est sans cesse à remettre en question.

37.   «Vous tenez là le discours d'une coquette», dit à Hortense une amie à vocation pédagogique. Ce discours révèle de fait une assez grande prétention («Quoique jeune, je
connais tout le danger d'un engagement»), discours leurré qui s'essaie maladroitement
à être leurrant.

38.   Pour Mme de Théville, voir p. 143:

C'était une femme assez belle encore, mais dont la physionomie était haute et
n'annonçait pas beaucoup de douceur dans le caractère.

Voir aussi la *froide* réponse de la mère à son fils qui avoue son intérêt pour Hortense.
Au reste, les deux femmes sont en froid.

39.   On remarquera que la quête désespérée du plaisir est aussi un trait de Mme de
Sénanges et qu'elle est ironiquement qualifiée de «femme philosophe». Meilcour traite
Versac de «philosophe»: «Je vous trouve philosophe, vous ! [...] Cessez de vous en
étonner, interrompit-il[...]» (208). Ce sont les deux seuls emplois du terme.

40.   L'opération n'est possible que parce que Versac n'y risque pas le duel avec l'homme
de Mme de Lursay. Laclos l'a fort bien perçu.

41.   Sur cette question de la pluralité d'objet, je renvoie à mon étude: «Esthétique et
libertinage: l'amour de l'art et l'art d'aimer». *Eros philosophe*, pub. par F. Moureau,
Slatkine, 1985.

42.

> Vous avez actuellement besoin d'une femme qui vous mette dans le monde, et
> c'est moi qui y mets toutes celles qui veulent y être célèbres. (207–08)

43. On remarquera du reste que dans la philosophie de Versac l'intérêt qu'il manifeste au jeune Meilcour est parfaitement inexplicable. Est-ce le signe qu'il occupe une position intenable et qu'il cède à la tentation de se montrer tel qu'il est, comme Don Juan parlant, faute de mieux, à Sganarelle?

44. Cette approche synthétique de l'auparavant me semble se produire dans *l'Arlequin poli par l'amour* de Marivaux, matrice d'un mythe, et se traduire par l'incertitude sur l'âge du personnage.

45. On rappellera, pour ne pas simplifier les choses,

    i. que l'œuvre est dédié au père de l'auteur, dont l'éclat est indiscutable; et

    ii. que l'auteur des *Egarements* naquit quinze jours après le mariage de ses parents.

PATRICIA LOUETTE

Quelques aspects de la singularité féminine chez Mme de Tencin: les coulisses de la vertu

Les héroïnes de Mme de Tencin sont des êtres singuliers à plus d'un titre. Elles apparaissent comme des victimes qui subissent les cruautés les plus diverses: parents, époux, amants, confidentes s'y entendent fort bien pour les tyranniser. A cela s'ajoutent les préjugés sociaux, le poids d'un devoir qu'elles semblent ne jamais oublier, les conséquences d'une éducation mal faite et la tentation de l'amour. Rien de très neuf dans tout cela, sauf peut-être cette manière d'occuper, presque à la fois, tout le champ des contraintes: on peut déjà y voir l'indice d'une ironie discrète de la part d'une romancière qui donne à voir des héroïnes qui en font un peu trop.

Mais la singularité des héroïnes s'exprime d'abord dans ce que nous pourrions appeler une trajectoire inattendue: celles qui se présentent comme des personnes vertueuses au début de leur histoire en viennent, après l'expérience de la soumission la plus rigoureuse bien souvent, à se comporter en personnages subversifs qui minent l'ordre établi.

Nous examinerons le destin de ces femmes[1] qui pratiquent consciemment, à des degrés divers, ce que Mme de Charrière a nommé «une morale un peu relâchée»[2] (Adélaïde et Eugénie méritent plus d'attention que les autres, à cet égard). Une expérience qui mène parfois à un héroïsme féminin, dans un univers où les personnages masculins peinent à devenir des héros.

Nous questionnerons donc cette singularité, dans une perspective freudienne, chez les héroïnes qui présentent des trajectoires ou des destinées en lignes brisées, et tenterons de (ré)évaluer, par-delà les effets de discontinuité que cela suppose, noirceur, grandeur, générosité et passion féminines.

Mlle de Glocester, l'héroïne de la première histoire des *Anecdotes*[3], est une ingénue élevée loin de la cour (comme la princesse de Clèves[4]), séduite par

Gaveston, figure de libertin qui la berne par des protestations de fidélité alors qu'il la trompe avec la maîtresse de son frère et qu'il courtise ouvertement la reine Isabelle. Mais Mlle de Glocester ne se comporte pas, comme on pouvait s'y attendre: la jeune fille inexpérimentée en vient à dispenser des conseils à son amant qui en disent long sur le savoir-faire du personnage féminin. Investie d'un rôle pédagogique, elle incarne une bonne mère, ou un mentor, à l'égard de Gaveston, en enseignant à l'homme de cour un comportement que la sociabilité exige de lui, en tentant de le polir (au sens où la fée «polit» Arlequin[5]). Mlle de Glocester, paradoxalement, est dépositaire d'un savoir qu'elle acquiert grâce aux expériences de son amant (qui lui n'est pas capable d'ériger en savoir ses expériences politiques et amoureuses). Autrement dit, le rôle intellectuel est dévolu à la femme: c'est elle qui élabore, en véritable tacticienne, la politique des relations qu'il doit entretenir auprès de la reine. On relève aussi que la position de maîtrise de l'héroïne débouche sur une véritable générosité: elle ne cède pas à la jalousie en perdant ses illusions et conserve sa bienveillance à l'égard de l'être aimé.

Alors que Gaveston n'est pas susceptible d'évolution intérieure (il reste irresponsable), l'héroïne montre un trajet dynamique qui mène de l'enfance ingénue à une maturité précoce et généreuse. Et il apparaît finalement que la naïveté est du côté du libertin et que le rapport de maîtrise et de savoir est du côté de l'ingénue.

La seconde histoire des *Anecdotes* désigne une trajectoire féminine problématique. Le narrateur (Saint-Martin) laisse entrevoir «la plus noire des perfid[e]s» (52): à l'âge de 12 ans, Mlle de Lascy tombe amoureuse de lui, sans le savoir (il est alors son précepteur). Cette Agnès ne répond que «par des pleurs» (27) timides aux volontés inflexibles de Lascy, père «impérieux et dur» (26), qui veut lui faire épouser un personnage odieux nommé Lancastre (au mieux mari geôlier, au pire assassin de sa première épouse). A 14 ans, elle se décide à épouser secrètement son amant et à le suivre en France. Or, le jour du départ, au comble de la félicité, Saint-Martin fait l'objet d'une tentative d'assassinat et est laissé pour mort (le héros, pour échapper aux poursuites de ses assaillants, accepte de passer pour mort). Cette trahison est orchestrée, selon Forville (fidèle serviteur du narrateur) par la jeune épouse elle-même, pour des motifs qui resteront mystérieux (le roman étant inachevé). Survient ensuite le mariage de l'héroïne avec Lancastre. Elle a 15 ans, à ce moment-là.

Voilà une existence bien remplie, riche en éléments compromettants: elle a désobéi à son père en épousant Saint-Martin; elle est bigame (puisque Saint-Martin est encore vivant); elle est (peut-être) une meurtrière. Et que penser de ce mariage avec Lancastre auquel elle a (mystérieusement) consenti, alors que son engagement avec Saint-Martin devait l'en dispenser? Il y a quelque chose d'inquiétant dans ce vœu de mort féminin qui succède aux premières relations sexuelles, faisant de l'héroïne une espèce de mante religieuse.

Quelle jeune fille terrifiante si l'on adopte le point de vue du narrateur: Saint-Martin croyait la sauver d'un mariage sordide et la soustraire à l'emprise d'un père scandaleusement ambitieux, et il est peut-être l'objet d'une machination féminine dont le lecteur, avec lui, ne connaît pas le dernier mot. Est-il manœuvré de bout en bout par l'héroïne[6]? Se laisse-t-il aveugler par des apparences qui sont contre elle?

Mme de Tencin souligne la bizarrerie de ce destin féminin à travers une succession de moments d'extase et de désespoir. Mais cette trajectoire en ligne brisée renvoie peut-être, autant que les *Mémoires du comte de Comminge*[7] (1735), à la défaillance de l'amant. Le texte met en avant une possible crédulité qui mettrait en question la crédibilité du narrateur: si le serviteur conserve la confiance de son maître, il n'en va pas de même pour l'héroïne.

En effet, c'est sur la foi du rapport de Forville que Saint-Martin la condamne sans retour[8], après avoir obtenu d'elle les plus grandes preuves d'amour. Le «caractère incompréhensible des femmes» (pour répéter Renoncour à propos de Manon[9]) repose ici sur un manque absolu de confiance en l'être aimé: le rapport du domestique pourrait être faux (comme celui de l'espion paternel dans le premier roman publié de Mme de Tencin[10]) ou bien incomplet et déformé (le prince de Clèves s'y laisse prendre lors de l'épisode de Coulommiers).

Si la cruauté de Mlle de Lascy reste indécidable, l'adhésion de Saint-Martin à l'accusation portée contre sa femme laisse supposer une inconstance qui pourrait bien dissimuler un désir agressif inconscient[11].

Pauline rapporte la vie de sa confidente Eugénie à l'intérieur de ses propres mémoires, intitulés *Les Malheurs de l'amour*[12] (1747). L'héroïne secondaire connaît une évolution remarquable dans le récit premier et dans le récit intercalé.

Cette religieuse Eugénie est dépositaire d'une conscience morale qui fait défaut aux parents de Pauline. En ce sens, elle incarne aux yeux de Pauline une bonne mère à laquelle la narratrice accorde toute sa confiance (elle réclame d'ailleurs son assentiment pour ses premières amours). Au couvent, Eugénie prend spontanément la défense de Pauline enfant, victime du préjugé de naissance. Or, ce personnage positif en vient à trahir sa protégée: elle pousse Barbasan, à l'insu de Pauline, mais pour son bien, à se détourner d'elle. La voix qui dénigre la passion, dans la tradition de *La Princesse de Clèves*, le fait au nom de raisons plus personnelles que morales. Le mentor de Pauline est donc un personnage aussi trouble que ceux qui peuplent les romans de Prévost: indépendamment de cette trahison qui rappelle l'attitude répressive de la mère de Pauline, Eugénie pousse l'héroïne à épouser d'Hacqueville, pour se venger de Barbasan qui lui est infidèle[13], alors qu'elle-même regrette d'avoir suivi des conseils analogues (on relève ici un procédé de mise en abîme). Comment justifier une telle démarche? Il y a là l'indice d'une agressivité qu'il convient de mettre en rapport avec sa propre histoire — édifiante, à cet égard.

Eugénie y connaît une trajectoire plus singulière encore: sacrifiée au profit d'un frère aîné (ce qu'elle ignore), l'héroïne (nommée Mlle d'Essei, puis Joyeuse) tente d'échapper au couvent grâce à une protectrice, Mme de Polignac. Sous sa direction, l'aristocrate pauvre ne perd pas de temps: en chemin pour Paris, où elle se rend pour trouver un parti, elle séduit le riche et puissant Blanchefort qui se déclare à mi-mot[14]. Un autre prétendant d'égale condition, La Valette, surgit dès son arrivée à Paris; elle ménage les deux intrigues à la fois, mais à la première déconvenue avec La Valette (qu'elle aime pourtant) elle épouse Blanchefort[15], par dépit. L'amour-propre d'Eugénie est plus impatient que celui de la Julie de Mme d'Aulnoy[16] (1690) dans une situation analogue. Cette précipitation suspecte, qui renforce l'image d'une femme intéressée, s'avère être une très mauvaise opération: Blanchefort l'abandonne, par ambition, alors qu'elle est enceinte. Et lorsqu'elle revendique la validité de leur union, Blanchefort la traite comme une courtisane qu'il convient de dédommager.

Or il se trouve que cette femme vouée aux plus honteuses humiliations, on l'apprend à la fin de son histoire, est aussi «la plus grande héritière de France» (60), nommée, par une ironie assez cruelle, *Joyeuse* (fille de joie?). Le dénouement de ce récit laisse encore pointer l'humour de Mme de Tencin: celle qui risque tout pour échapper au couvent devient religieuse de plein gré, et son insistance à l'être égale sa détermination antérieure à ne l'être pas. Il est aussi savoureux, dans un autre ordre d'idées, de voir que la fille du peuple (Hippolyte, rivale de Pauline) connaît un destin moins scabreux, dans ce roman, que la grande aristocrate...

L'aristocrate vient donc incarner — et ceci n'ôte rien à l'odieux mari — la scandaleuse disponibilité d'une jeune fille contrariée dans ses aspirations sociales: Blanchefort remplace aisément La Valette; la mort de son fils lui permet, selon elle, de prononcer des vœux du vivant de Blanchefort.

Mais la situation précaire d'Eugénie n'aboutit pas au choix de Manon. L'héroïne de Mme de Tencin prétend à l'estime et à la vertu.

Blanchefort, lui, ramène, sans beaucoup de scrupule, sa passion pour elle à une expérience sensuelle dont elle ne doit plus rien attendre (hormis des compensations qui l'indignent): il n'a pas besoin d'éprouver de l'estime à son égard (les conditions de leur rencontre entament par avance toute considération de cet ordre); quant à l'estime qu'elle prétend lui retirer, il n'en a que faire (seule celle qu'il tient de ses pairs lui importe).

Le mariage garantit la vertu et lui permet de faire l'impasse sur l'expérience de la prostitution à laquelle elle se livre (sa protectrice qui la jette dans les bras du premier venu[17], s'apparente à une mère maquerelle). Quand la perspective du mariage a disparu (nul doute que le «perfide» (37) qui en détruit les preuves est Blanchefort!), il ne reste rien pour idéaliser une démarche intéressée. Or, quoi de plus légitime au fond? Elle n'a pas le choix, pour échapper au couvent, d'une voie plus digne. L'instance d'énonciation fait percevoir une certaine hypocrisie chez l'héroïne: le rôle de «suppliante» (59) qu'elle s'inflige auprès de son perfide (ce registre tragique laisse supposer à Blanchefort qu'elle est passionnée) est une humiliation imposée au *moi* de l'héroïne qui lave, en somme,

de l'infamie de la prostitution, tout en permettant un possible retour du mari...
La soumission féminine cache des intentions que le personnage ne reconnaît pas
pour siennes mais que le texte tend à désigner comme telles à travers des choix
et des actes.

Mais la vertu sert implicitement des motifs moins louables: l'ambition et
la revanche.

L'héroïne entend vivre assez rapidement comme une femme épousée dans
des conditions normales et ne pas jouer le jeu du mariage secret durablement
(ceci pointe avant la trahison de Blanchefort); son orgueil la tyrannise, excepté
durant la période de répit imposé par la mort de sa protectrice. Sa grossesse ne
fait que hâter une exigence de reconnaissance officielle, à laquelle elle tient
beaucoup (Eugénie n'est pas la Silvie de Challes[18]). La revanche qu'elle prendrait sur Mlle de Magnelais (sa rivale auprès de La Valette) l'a poussée à risquer,
pauvreté oblige (du moins, le croit-elle avec le lecteur) le mariage secret[19]. D'où
son impatience de figurer à la cour.

Si donc elle souffre réellement d'une situation malheureuse (mari perfide,
amant incapable, parents cupides), sa façon d'y répondre n'atteint pas la dignité
qu'elle revendique après coup. Mais il lui importe de conserver une haute idée
d'elle-même (sa grande naissance ne fera que la confirmer), car cette estime de
soi, fondée sur une vertu assez vaine, la maintient en vie. Son narcissisme initial
(flatté par Mme de Polignac, gonflé par les circonstances) parvient à triompher
des vœux de mort qui se font entendre[20], au prix d'un dégoût pour le monde, et
au-delà pour les autres. Il en résulte un amour du *moi* pour lui-même, au détri-
ment des objets: elle renonce à La Valette une seconde fois alors qu'elle le sait
innocent, elle accable Blanchefort honteux d'un mépris dont elle fut jadis victime (il en meurt). Triomphe d'un narcissisme agressif, voire sadique, dont
Pauline fera aussi les frais (à travers les conseils reçus).

Il n'est pas indifférent pour nous que ce triomphe se produise chez une
aristocrate. Mlle de Joyeuse est une héroïne qui, malgré sa naissance, ne connaît
jamais la grandeur. Des amoureuses venues de ce monde ignoble des *lingères*, des
filles de boutiques ou des *finances* l'incarnent à sa place. Hippolyte et Pauline ou
la grandeur d'une fille de geôlier racinienne et d'une fille de partisan corné-
lienne. Ceci est à mettre en rapport avec la parole de l'aristocrate confisquée:

Pauline, narratrice, laisse Hippolyte se raconter tandis qu'elle narre l'histoire d'Eugénie à la troisième personne. Le roman a rarement compromis aussi radicalement le prestige de la (plus grande) noblesse...

Qu'en est-il de la trajectoire féminine dans les *Mémoires du comte de Comminge?* Adélaïde de Lussan ne peut épouser son amant en raison d'une haine familiale qui oppose son père à Comminge, père du narrateur, à propos d'un héritage (procès, duel). Comminge est prêt à tout pour les séparer (il emprisonne son fils, calomnie Adélaïde, etc.). L'héroïne, pour libérer son amant, envisage de se marier (puisque c'est la condition imposée par Comminge père). Mme de Comminge, *mère confidente* aussi trouble que sa sœur marivaudienne (1735), avouera à son fils que c'est elle-même qui l'y a déterminée. A la surprise générale, Adélaïde épouse le plus odieux de ses prétendants[21], Bénavidès, pour signifier son sacrifice (elle le confesse au narrateur dans une lettre à laquelle, il faut bien le dire, il ne comprend rien). Comminge désespéré la rejoint, malgré l'interdiction d'Adélaïde, et se fait surprendre aux pieds de la belle par le mari jaloux. Le furieux tente de la tuer, est blessé gravement par Comminge touché lui aussi. Le frère de Bénavidès, Gabriel, amoureux d'Adélaïde, sauve Comminge des poursuites menées contre lui. Réfugié dans une abbaye, Comminge veut s'enfermer à la Trappe lorsque Gabriel lui apprend la mort d'Adélaïde. Trois ans après ses vœux, il assiste à la mort d'un trappiste qui se confesse publiquement: c'est Adélaïde, devenue veuve, que son mari a fait passer pour morte pour mieux exercer sa vengeance. Travestie en homme, elle a choisi de rester au couvent dès qu'elle y reconnaît son amant, pour vivre à ses côtés, sans se découvrir (elle le croit converti à Dieu). Elle meurt repentante dans les bras de son amant. Comminge, désespéré, devient ermite et se met à écrire ses mémoires.

Avant d'aborder les aspects troubles de la singularité d'Adélaïde, évoquons brièvement les procédés de mise en relief du personnage féminin. Sa singularité se manifeste d'abord par ce nom qu'elle porte dans un univers peuplé de noms historiques (Comminge, Foix, La Valette, etc.), et par ce qui passe, au début des *Mémoires*, pour une intrusion d'un élément féminin dans une généalogie exclusivement masculine (le narrateur y néglige absolument les femmes): «qu'une fille» prend ici toute sa saveur[22]. Elle est encore le personnage qui meurt d'amour alors que c'est elle qui semblait renoncer à la passion.

Elle prend la parole (longuement) dans des mémoires qui ne sont pas les siens. Son discours, qui met en scène une mort spectaculaire, décide de la rédaction, de l'existence du texte (Comminge après la (fausse) nouvelle de sa mort n'entreprend pas d'écrire).

Le terme *singulier*, pour elle, se rapproche de celui de *solitaire*: soupçonnée d'adultère par Bénavidès, d'inconstance par Comminge, de perfidie par Comminge père (sur les calomnies d'un espion), elle doit se battre sur tous les fronts de la violence et de la tendresse (Mme de Comminge et Gabriel non exceptés).

Singulière, elle l'est aussi par cette manière particulière qu'elle a d'incarner une victime exemplaire, et nous abordons ici les aspects inquiétants de sa singularité.

La «criminelle» (92) qu'elle est devenue a peu de rapport avec cette héroïne vertueuse qui apparaissait au début des *Mémoires*, et qui, attentive à son devoir, repoussait avec indignation la proposition d'enlèvement de Comminge; qui, une fois mariée, le conjure de ne plus chercher à la voir, et qui refuse, malgré les mauvais traitements qui l'attendent, la fuite que lui propose Gabriel. A quoi bon refuser tout cela pour en arriver là?

Si l'on songe que le roman est court et ne contient qu'un nombre restreint d'événements (qui concernent d'ailleurs plus Comminge qu'elle-même), le parcours d'Adélaïde prend un relief particulier: le choix suspect de l'époux odieux intervient quelques mois seulement après la rencontre amoureuse (laquelle s'accompagne de déclarations morales) et le séjour sacrilège à la Trappe se situe après «deux ans» (89) d'enfermement conjugal. En l'espace de trois petites années, Adélaïde donne à voir une trajectoire remarquable par le changement qui s'opère.

Or, la soumission au devoir, affirmée au début des *Mémoires*, ne cesse d'être rappelée[23] par l'héroïne elle-même, et ce mariage dénoncé dans la confession finale («contracté par des vues si criminelles» (88)) passe l'examen de la conscience morale lorsqu'elle se confie à Gabriel:

> je n'ai fait aucune démarche que le plus rigoureux devoir puisse condamner.
> (80)

Passons sur ce qui peut être considéré comme une équivoque.[24] Plus grave est cette certitude affirmée (33) et réaffirmée, que les événements et sa confession viendront démentir, de ne jamais faillir:

> ma tendresse peut me rendre malheureuse [...] mais elle ne me rendra jamais criminelle. (42)

Or elle dénonce à la Trappe sa «passion criminelle» (92) qui l'a poussée à *profaner* (88) de «saints lieux» et à *blasphémer* (90).

Le programme vertueux qu'elle propose à Comminge est mis en question:

> quoiqu'il arrive, promettons-nous de ne rien faire qui puisse nous faire rougir l'un de l'autre. (42)

La confession d'Adélaïde vient infirmer ces grandes déclarations morales. Si l'on remarque avec J. Decottignies que l'amant, fort peu estimable, ne respecte pas ce pacte, on ne peut manquer de constater qu'Adélaïde en fait autant.

Curieux aussi cet intérêt pour l'estime des autres. S'il est légitime de demander celle de l'amant et de prétendre à la sienne propre, l'estime de Bénavidès (81) et Mme de Comminge (53) explicitement revendiquée paraît, en revanche, suspecte[25].

Le projet est d'autant plus surprenant que cette mère est une alliée du père odieux, manipulatrice qui ne dit pas son nom et qui exerce un chantage sur l'héroïne pour qu'elle se marie. La vertu est poussée un peu loin puisqu'il s'agit de gagner l'estime de la mère de l'amant en incarnant l'épouse vertueuse d'un mari qui n'entretient aucune espèce de rapport avec Mme de Comminge.

Quant à l'estime du mari, rien ne paraît plus exagéré. Bénavidès n'est pas le prince de Clèves (ne serait-ce que parce qu'il a été choisi), il ne demande pas à l'être d'ailleurs et son caractère l'exclut absolument: c'est bien là un *fantôme de devoir* que s'invente l'héroïne et qui donne à voir un *surmoi* tyrannisant le *moi*. La hantise du devoir, à travers laquelle se perçoit l'humour de la romancière, est ici poussée jusqu'à l'absurde.

On peut se demander d'ailleurs jusqu'à quel point ce devoir est pris au sérieux: Adélaïde a épousé Bénavidès pour donner «une espèce de fidélité» (47) à son amant et garde le «petit chien» (56) offert par Comminge, symbole de fidélité dans la tradition courtoise. Par ailleurs, on s'approche, dans les *Mémoires*, de ce «personnage de suppliante» qu'Eugénie joue auprès de son mari, mais l'hypocrisie avouée dans les *Malheurs*, reste ici indécidable:

> quoiqu'il se fût obstiné à ne la point voir, quelque instance qu'elle lui en eût fait faire dans le plus fort de son mal, il demandait de ses nouvelles [...]. (83)

On saura, d'après la confession finale, que l'hypocrisie est du côté masculin (puisque c'est une feinte de Bénavidès). Mais Adélaïde ne se prononce pas sur la sienne.

L'héritage classique est ainsi désigné (les contemporains y ont été sensibles) tout en étant discrètement corrigé: Adélaïde peut prétendre jusqu'à un certain point à «l'innocence» (81) (l'amant a mis en cause inconsidérément sa réputation d'épouse vertueuse), mais l'estime du mari qu'elle exige est de trop, assurément. Son innocence, à tous les sens du terme, n'en dépend pas.

Il se cache peut-être derrière cette motivation du devoir une volonté suicidaire (le devoir conjugal serait alors l'équivalent des exercices mortifères des trappistes). «Je ne sais si M. de Bénavidès en veut à mes jours» dit-elle à Gabriel (78). Or elle vient d'en avoir la preuve puisqu'il a déjà attenté à sa vie. Et elle refuse, par «devoir», la fuite proposée:

> Je le remplirais quoi qu'il puisse m'en coûter. (78)

Sujétion immorale de la femme à l'époux? Rien n'est tenté du vivant de Bénavidès (travestissement et fuite interviennent *après* sa mort). Or le roman envisage volontiers cette solution depuis la fin du XVIIème siècle; on trouve même des exemples dans la vie des Grands: Hortense Mancini fuit, comme Henriette-Sylvie de Molière, l'héroïne de Mme de Villedieu (1671–74), sous un déguisement masculin, les persécutions d'un époux. Adélaïde, elle, se contente de dénoncer son enfer conjugal: on peut y lire la marque d'une inhibition qui vient contredire performances et héroïsme antérieurs. Que paye-t-elle donc ici? Le choix de Bénavidès (le texte s'y attarde plusieurs fois) repose sur son indignité même (mauvaise humeur, laideur, jalousie, «peu d'esprit»[26] (52); il ne possède que le titre de marquis), et c'est moins la passion pour un autre qui est en jeu, sur un plan fantasmatique, que l'horreur qu'il inspire à l'héroïne. Bénavidès lui promet, indépendamment de la catastrophe provoquée par la visite de Comminge, l'avenir le plus sombre; la motivation de ne pas donner de jalousie à son amant, accompagne le désir de supporter, en toute connaissance de cause, un objet qui ne lui est pas indifférent, contrairement à ce qu'elle affirme[27] : «celui qui ne pouvait m'inspirer que de la haine fut préféré» (88). Le geste est beau, généreux assurément (elle libère Comminge et répond majestueusement au sacrifice des titres brûlés par lui[28]: «les fureurs de M. de Comminge m'ont instruite de ce que je vous dois» (47)). Mais Bénavidès est la victime de ce manège (ce qui ne le rend pas sympathique pour autant évidemment); il y a donc l'indice d'une agressivité à l'encontre du prétendant.

Peur devant le désir? Eugénie se moquait de Pauline lorsqu'on ne lui donnait pas Barbasan. Elle ajoutait que sa peine ne serait pas éternelle... (L'horizon d'un bonheur possible avec d'Hacqueville vient confirmer furtivement cette éventualité). Devant la possibilité (très humaine) d'investir un autre objet d'amour, l'héroïne concevrait un dégoût d'elle-même qui ne lui permettrait plus de s'estimer (la grande passion exige peut-être cela). Bénavidès, l'homme repoussant par excellence, constitue le rempart le plus solide à cette tentation de se savoir aimée, mieux aimée que par Comminge lui-même. Le danger ne vient plus de l'être aimé, comme la Princesse le laissait entendre, mais du sujet amoureux lui-même.

Cette tentation figure dans le roman sous les traits de Gabriel. Il devient amoureux d'Adélaïde alors qu'il aime ailleurs. Cet amant signifie que le désir surgit, sans crier gare, chez les êtres les plus vertueux (il l'est et le lui montre; son attitude est chevaleresque à un point que n'atteindra jamais Comminge). L'investissement sur un autre objet d'amour est assumé par le héros masculin le plus respectueux à l'égard des injonctions de la Dame. Adélaïde peut reconnaître en lui une image du désir qui la renvoie à son propre rapport à Comminge et à la tentation dont elle s'est préservée, de fait, en épousant Bénavidès.

Il faut mettre en rapport cette situation avec le scénario œdipien. Bénavidès, réplique de Comminge père, est le contraire de l'amant, mais il est aussi le contraire de Lussan.

Le père d'Adélaïde est «naturellement [...] doux» (22); Comminge père est «naturellement emporté» (34). Le narrateur tend implicitement à reconnaître en Lussan un modèle positif (même victoire généreuse lors du duel; la «mélancolie» (43, 53) de l'amant fait écho à cette douceur[29]). On y reconnaît là l'indice d'une identification bien plus qualifiante, selon le point de vue de Comminge, que celle entrevue à l'égard de son propre père[30] et qui fait l'objet d'une dénégation.

Mais Lussan père, valorisé par le narrateur, est curieusement absent de la vie de la jeune fille: il est incapable de la mettre à l'abri des persécutions diffamatoires de son cousin et des manœuvres de Mme de Comminge. Lussan reste choqué par l'attitude de Comminge père mais n'entreprend aucune démarche pour soutenir l'honneur de sa fille; le duel qui lave le sien lui suffit. Il pousse Adélaïde à se marier mais il n'a aucune autorité sur elle (52) puisqu'elle s'y refuse jusqu'à ce qu'elle se décide pour Bénavidès (décision sur laquelle le père ne se manifeste à aucun moment). Lussan n'est donc pas un bon père; il ne l'est que par contraste, quand il est comparé à Comminge père.

L'inhibition de l'amant, incapable de sauver sa maîtresse (il goûte les douceurs de la prison tandis que pèsent sur elle les menaces paternelles) fait écho à cette désinvolture — pour ne pas dire ce désintérêt — de Lussan à l'égard de sa fille. Même inconsistance de part et d'autre, même égoïsme aussi.

Est-ce suffisant pour admettre que l'amant est le substitut du père dans cette histoire et qu'en tant que tel il est un objet interdit à Adélaïde?

Epouser Bénavidès (double de Comminge père), c'est garantir à l'amant qu'elle n'aime que lui, mais c'est aussi indiquer à Lussan qu'elle se choisit un objet haï du père: un mari qui ne volera pas l'amour de la fille pour le père. L'attitude d'Adélaïde envers Bénavidès serait donc la trace d'une culpabilité liée à un choix d'objet de type incestueux. Cette recherche effrénée de l'estime, relevée à propos du mari et de Mme de Comminge, pourrait trouver là son explication.

La démarche finale d'Adélaïde et sa confession publique viennent s'inscrire à l'issue d'une trajectoire insolite en elle-même. Le dénouement n'arrange rien. S'y confirme un idéal qui mine l'ordre établi: devoir, vertu, fidélité impliquent d'autres valeurs que celles partagées par l'ensemble des autres personnages (Comminge compris), Gabriel excepté. Le devoir est paradoxal (au sens où il s'oppose à la *doxa*), comme la vertu. La morale affirmée tout au long du roman par l'héroïne n'est autre que celle de la passion.

Ce qui singularise, en dernier lieu, Adélaïde, c'est l'amour. Sa passion est toute chevaleresque: c'est elle qui incarne le chevalier respectueux, discret, éprouvé de la littérature courtoise. Ce nom de romancière qu'elle porte renvoie au Moyen Âge[31] (cher à Marguerite de Lussan) et au rapport à l'amour qu'il suppose: des valeurs qu'ignore la nouvelle classique. Adélaïde ne connaît pas la jalousie obsédante (et hallucinée) de Mme de Clèves; elle ne se méprise pas d'aimer et ignore cet arrachement à elle-même que ressentent les héros classiques (dont Comminge) en tombant amoureux. Quant au repos, il est un sacrifice exigé par l'amour (47).

L'amour reste une expérience positive, absolue, dont Adélaïde affirme la toute puissance au sein même de la Trappe. Sa confession est sacrilège du point de vue de l'institution: le repentir reflue toujours vers le désir. Le plaisir qu'offre la formulation du désir ne compte pas pour rien (dénoncer le désir, c'est en parler) et Mme de Tencin s'amuse visiblement à placer le rappel jubilatoire de toutes les fautes dans un lieu où l'on fait vœu de silence. Et par-delà le spectacle subversif de ce repentir, c'est le «scandale» (93, 94) de toute espèce de confession qui est désigné.

Ce qui tue Adélaïde? L'indignité de ce chevalier manqué (faux «LongAUNOIS» (24): c'est sous ce nom qu'il se fait aimé d'elle). Les amants de Mme d'Aulnoy savaient prendre du bon temps au couvent[32] tandis que cet «ingrat» (93) n'y reconnaît pas Adélaïde. Comminge a renoncé à elle en tant qu'être charnel, en momifiant sa passion à la Trappe. Préférer le repos larmoyant à l'objet d'amour lui-même, au regard des valeurs chevaleresques, est une trahison, non pas sexuelle comme celle de Barbasan[33], mais une *espèce d'infidélité* infiniment plus grave: plus qu'Adélaïde, c'est sa passion qu'il aime. L'amante n'est pas la rivale de Dieu[34], mais celle du narcissisme de l'amant.

Adélaïde en perdra le goût de vivre. Et c'est bien parce qu'elle ne renonce pas à l'amour, qu'elle renonce à la vie.

L'humour transparent de Mme de Tencin laisse entrevoir un dernier sacrifice: la mort de l'héroïne laisse Comminge, en ermitage (l'austérité de la Trappe ne suffit plus...), à la jouissance de ses larmes et au plaisir de se raconter. C'est au nom de cela qu'elle en vient à rompre la loi du secret, si nécessaire aux amants de la tradition courtoise: la parole féminine vient autoriser la parole masculine et donne à Comminge le moyen de transformer une vie insignifiante en destin. D'en faire un roman, en somme.

UNIVERSITÉ DE PARIS III — SORBONNE NOUVELLE

NOTES

1.   On exclut, pour des questions de place, les héroïnes du *Siège de Calais* (1739). Je renvoie à R. Démoris pour le personnage de Mme de Granson: «De l'usage des noms propres: le roman historique au XVIIIème siècle», RHLF, 1975, n° 2–3, p. 268–288.

2.   *Le Noble, conte moral* (1763), Ed. J. Hellegouarch, LGF, 1994, p. 233.

3.   *Anecdotes de la cour et du règne d'Edouard II, roi d'Angleterre* (1776), Paris, d'Hautel, 1812 *(Anecdotes)*.

4.   Mme de Lafayette *La Princesse de Clèves* (1678).

5.   Marivaux *Arlequin poli par l'amour* (1720).

6.   La proposition de mariage secret répond à la demande qu'elle lui fait d'être conduite au couvent pour échapper à Lancastre.

7.   Edition citée: Desjonquères, 1996 *(Mémoires)*.

8.   Elle n'a jamais l'occasion de s'expliquer.

9.   Prévost *Manon Lescaut* (1731), Ed. F. Deloffre et R. Picart, Bordas, 1990, p. 15. Je renvoie à l'étude de R. Démoris, *Le Silence de Manon*, PUF, 1995, p. 14–15.

10. *Les Mémoires.*

11. Il songe à la poignarder quand il apprend cette trahison.

12. Edition citée: Paris, d'Hautel, 1812 *(Malheurs)*.

13.

> Je veux, me répondit-elle, que vous en fassiez votre vengeur, que vous vous amusiez de sa passion. (204)

14.   Ce que dit Masson de Barbasan et Hippolyte conviendrait aussi à Eugénie et
       Blanchefort: «divertissement dans un amour de grand chemin» dans *Mme de Tencin
       (1682-1749)*, Hachette, 1909, p. 144.

15.   Sa précarité explique sans doute cela, mais l'effet produit tend à relativiser une pas-
       sion qui se donne pour telle.

16.   *L'Histoire d'Hypolite, comte de Duglas*, edited with an Introduction in English and
       French by Shirley Jones Day, 1994, U. of London. Julie qui croit Hypolite marié
       veut épouser Bedfort: «je sacrifierai mon repos à mon amour-propre» (74).

17.   Blanchefort est le premier homme qu'elle rencontre!

18.   *Les Illustres françaises* (1713).

19.
              Un autre motif acheva de la déterminer, le plaisir d'être d'un rang égal à celui
              de Mlle de Magnelais: la différence que leur naissance avait mise entre elles ne
              l'avaient point touchée jusque-là; mais elle était humiliée depuis qu'elle savait
              l'amour de La Valette. (20)

20.   Blanchefort, Joyeuse père et mère; elle est aussi tentée par le suicide.

21.   Se reporter à J. Decottignies: Introduction à l'édition des *Mémoires*, Lille, Giard,
       1969; « Roman et revendication féministe d'après les *Mémoires* », *Roman et Lumières
       au XVIIIème siècle*, Ed. Sociales, 1970. Je ne souscris pas à l'ensemble des interpréta-
       tions (vision dix-neuvièmiste du mariage).

22.   «bisaïeul», «garçons», «frères», «cadet», «aîné», «père», «grand-père» (p. 21–22); «deux»
       (3 occurrences) s'oppose à «une».

23.   p. 33, 40, 42, 53, 64, 75, 78, 80, 81, 84, 89.

24.   L'orchestration de son mariage est sienne, mais Adélaïde ne se réfère ici qu'à sa vie
       d'épouse! Mme de Bénavidès, conformément à son programme vertueux, fuit une
       première fois Comminge puis le somme de partir quand il la surprend chez elle.

25.   «La crainte des discours que mon aventure ferait tenir de moi» (89) l'empêche de
       rétablir la vérité sur sa fausse mort. Redoute-t-elle ici de perdre ce qui serait l'estime
       du public?

26.   On sait quelle utilisation fait le roman des maris stupides!

27.
              Il ne m'importe [...] tout m'est égal puisque je ne puis être à celui à qui mon
              cœur s'était destiné. (52)

28.   Il s'agit de toute évidence d'une surenchère à la destruction des titres. Comminge n'y
       a pas grand-chose à perdre (une autre succession le rend plus riche que son père). A
       moins d'épouser le projet paternel...

29.   «ma mélancolie [...] avait cependant je ne sais quelle douceur» (53); «douceur des
      entretiens» amoureux (33), des larmes (42), le sacrifice des titres se présente comme le
      «moment [le] plus doux» (31).

30.   Vol et substitution du portrait, recours aux espions appartiennent au registre pater-
      nel; violence des persécutions amoureuses, discrètement signifiée: «elle voulut
      s'échapper [...] mais la retenant par la robe» (63).

31.   Mlle de Lussan *Anecdotes de Childéric* (1736) et surtout *Anecdotes de la cour de Philippe-
      Auguste* (1733–38): légende de la châtelaine de Vergy et de la belle *Adélaïde* de Coucy
      (tome 2, 1733). *Le Siège de Calais* montre l'intérêt de Mme de Tencin pour le Moyen
      Âge.

32.   *Hypolite*, éd. cit., p. 138, 140.

33.   On retrouve ce terme d'«ingrat» sous la plume de Pauline (73, 88, 197, 201).

34.   «Je blasphémai contre [Dieu] de me l'avoir ôté.» (90).

MARTIN HALL

Re-writing *La Princesse de Clèves*:
the *Anecdotes de la cour et du règne d'Edouard II*

One of the most important recent developments in eighteenth-century French studies has been the rediscovery of novels written by women who were acclaimed in their own time, but subsequently so neglected that by the twentieth century the memory of their work survived only in the footnotes of literary histories. Moreover, the revival of interest in their novels goes beyond mere literary palæontology. They now attract readers by their intrinsic merit, and by the challenge which they offer to settled notions of the novel-canon in the eighteenth century.[1] This article will be concerned with two novelists, who, in different degree, have been the object of renewed attention, Claudine-Alexandrine de Tencin and Anne-Louise de Beaumont.

The first is the better known of the two, although her status as a novelist has until recently been overshadowed by her reputation as one of the eighteenth century's most wayward and unconventional women.[2] She is the author of three completed novels, which are marked by their relatively conventional form and thematic material, but also by strange, subversive episodes and developments.[3]

The second novelist, Mme Elie de Beaumont, is less well known. She wrote only one complete novel, the *Lettres du Marquis de Roselle*, which appeared in 1764.[4] In contrast to Tencin, she acquired a reputation as a high-minded and devout woman.[5]

The connection between these novelists is Tencin's unfinished novel, the *Anecdotes de la cour et du règne d'Edouard II, roi d'Angleterre*. This remained unpublished at her death, and first appeared, with Beaumont's completion, in 1776.[6] The novel was poorly received and has been virtually ignored since its first appearance. Its derivativeness in part explains this neglect, for it belongs to a genre which had ceased to be fashionable by 1776, the 'galant' historical novel or *nouvelle*.[7] Yet this derivativeness constitutes the basis of the novel's claim on the modern reader's attention. This is most obvious in the climactic scene of the *Anecdotes* which is directly borrowed from a work published almost a century earlier, *La Princesse de Clèves*. In this scene, the heroine, recently widowed, grants an interview to the man who loved her when she was married, acknowledges his love for her, confesses that she feels for him 'des sentimens plus tendres que l'estime' (364), but rejects his offer of marriage. Both the Tencin and Beaumont episodes of the *Anecdotes* contain other reminiscences of *La Princesse de Clèves*, which illustrate the latter work's abiding influence on eighteenth-century novelists.

The full story of this influence lies beyond the scope of this article, but the path which takes us from the climactic interview of the *Anecdotes* to that in *La Princesse de Clèves* throws into relief one of the most important figures which this work bequeathed to later novelists, the figure of the widow. Mme de Lafayette did not, of course, 'invent' this figure, and it is one whose fictional potential exceeded what any single writer might encompass. Many of the most interesting and original heroines of *ancien régime* literature, from Molière's Célimène to Marivaux's Araminte and on to Laclos's Merteuil, are widows, and the literary prominence of the widow no doubt reflected a social reality of the period, and explained its attraction for these and other writers: widows were more likely than unmarried or married women to be in a position to control their own life, and to act autonomously. Our particular concern will be with one avatar of the widow, outstandingly represented by the Princess. What characterizes this particular representation of the widow is the importance which attaches to the moment of choice which follows bereavement, when, Janus-like, she looks back on her married past, and contemplates her future, before taking her destiny in her own hands.

Tencin's tale

In spite of its title, the *Anecdotes de la cour et du règne d'Edouard II* is not primarily concerned with Edward II, nor with his court. The historical context is the rise and fall of Edward's favourite, Piers Gaveston, but their relationship is not explored. Nor is Gaveston himself the central figure of the novel; this is 'Mademoiselle de Glocester', whom history remembers as the wife of Gaveston. In a manner typical of the 'galant' historical novel, a fairly well known historical episode is re-focussed in such a way that a woman, to whom 'serious' history grants only a very marginal role, becomes the primary focus of attention.[8] However, Gaveston's career provides the basic plot. In broad conformity with the historical record, he is presented as a very flawed 'hero', physically attractive, generous and courageous, but selfish, arrogant and impetuous. His personality is thrown into relief by contrast with the other leading male character, the Comte de Pembrocke, his unsuccessful rival for the heroine's affections.[9] He is reliable, sensitive, caring, loyal, but the impressive list of his virtues weighs little against Gaveston's dangerous charm. The contrast between the two suggests an obvious model, that of Nemours and Clèves in *La Princesse de Clèves*. Gaveston, indeed, is almost a caricature of Nemours, inheriting all the most suspect traits of the earlier hero, whilst Pembrocke is a stylized copy of Clèves, much less *nuancé*, and more the conventional courtly lover.[10] We need not suppose any direct inspiration from *La Princesse de Clèves*, since a contrasted pair of men is a constant in much of the feminocentric fiction of the 'galant' historical novel. Such fiction regularly presents a heroine caught between a man she loves but cannot marry, and a husband or fiancé whom she cannot love. Indeed, the 'ugly' male imposed by society and parents and the unobtainable but desirable male, as a pair, symbolize one of the fundamental conflicts which the genre articulates, between woman's desire and society's *diktat*. What is distinctive in Tencin's exploitation of this contrasted pair is the reversal of the usual roles: it is almost always the case that the unattractive male will end up as the husband, the more attractive one as the lost and regretted love. By contrast, in the Tencin tale, the heroine is heading towards marriage with the man of her desire.

As important as the presentation of a flawed hero is the heroine's emotional development as she falls under Gaveston's sway. There are three aspects to this development. Firstly, the heroine is aware of the flaws in Gaveston's personality from the start of their relationship, and becomes progressively more conscious of them. Secondly, she is ever more deeply attracted to him in spite of mounting evidence of his untrustworthiness. Thirdly, she becomes increasingly aware, not only that her emotional investment in their relationship is greater than his, but also that she is seeking to compensate, by her greater investment, for a lack of emotional reciprocation. Above all, the distinctiveness of the Tencin heroine lies in her combination of lucidity and passivity: as her insight into her own and Gaveston's feelings develops, and more insistently urges her to end the relationship, so she finds herself drawn into greater commitment, seemingly in spite of herself.

Mademoiselle de Glocester experiences love as a disturbing journey towards self-discovery, in which a growing understanding of her emotions and of the dangers to which these expose her is counterbalanced by a growing incapacity to act upon this understanding.[11] As in the presentation of the hero, so with the heroine: Tencin takes up some of the most distinctive features of the Princesse de Clèves, and accentuates these. The result is a tantalisingly unfinished piece of work, with clear echoes of *La Princesse de Clèves*, but which imposed a strange task on any completer — to resolve a tale in which the heroine is heading for marriage to the Nemours rather than the Clèves figure.

The Beaumont completion

In her completion, Beaumont respects the basic framework of Tencin's plot and characters.[12] She introduces no new characters, and remains broadly faithful to the historical record in tracing the relationship between the heroine and Gaveston: they marry, with the approval and encouragement of the King, but their marriage is of relatively short duration, and ends with Gaveston's murder.

Like any completion, Beaumont's stands in a complex relationship to its original. She inherits a story which only deals with the heroine before marriage, and is obliged by the historical record to take this heroine on through marriage to widowhood. Which part of the heroine's life she chose to explore is the pointer to where her interests lie, and it is soon obvious that these are not with the heroine's married life. She hurries through this in such scant detail that the most distinctive feature of the Tencin *Anecdotes*, its focus on the heroine's relationship with Gaveston and on the difference between male and female affectivity, is scarcely developed in the completion.

Beaumont's *Anecdotes*, it might be said, only truly begins with her heroine's widowhood. And with this widowhood, we come upon the only major falsification of history in the novel. Her bereaved heroine rejects Pembrocke's offer of marriage, and lives on, without remarrying, to extreme old age,[13] whereas the historical original was remarried to a relatively obscure knight called Hugh de Audley, probably for politico-dynastic reasons.[14] The suppression of this second marriage is noteworthy, because so contrary to the usual strategy of the 'galant' historical novelists. The 'second-marriage' plot, a relatively common one in their novels, typically took some twice-married princess or heiress as heroine. In conformity with the historical record, her first marriage would be presented as a loveless one, imposed for politico-dynastic reasons, usually by paternal coercion. The fictional heroine would nobly repress her feelings, almost invariably her love for the man who subsequently becomes her second husband. The second marriage would then be transformed into a 'happy ending' of emotional fulfilment — the dutiful heroine, after sacrificing herself to her father's or brother's will, would be allowed to escape into private bliss with the man of her choice.[15] The historical record offered Beaumont such a 'happy ending', and she rejected it. Clearly, we must take into account major differences between the plot which she inherited, and that elaborated in the typical 'second-marriage' novel. Two constants which defined the latter were absent from the Tencin tale: the heroine's being coerced into the first marriage, and her distaste for the husband imposed on her. Significantly, Beaumont seeks to restore just these elements in her completion. The heroine's acceptance of Gaveston as a husband is presented as the result of emotional blackmail,[16] whilst their married life is presented negatively, as one of growing mutual alienation. Indifferent to the relationship which formed the basis of the Tencin tale, Beaumont drives her heroine's tale towards the aftermath of bereavement, when the heroine makes her choice. Disdainful of the 'happy ending' which the historical record allowed her, she resorts to the model offered her by the final interview of *La Princesse de Clèves* to present a heroine who is defined as heroine by an act of refusal.

Bereavement

In exploiting the Clèves-Nemours interview, Beaumont makes a major change to it: she splits it into two interviews, the first with the heroine's brother (whose role at this stage approximates to that of the Vidame de Chartres), and the second with Pembrocke. Where past and future are discussed throughout the course of the single interview in *La Princesse de Clèves*, Beaumont assigns each to a distinct interview. In the first, the heroine is concerned to explain the past, in the second, with Pembrocke, her future is the primary issue. This division also highlights the fundamentally conflictual relationship that exists between the Tencin *Anecdotes* and its completion: the first interview radically reorientates the Tencin tale, whilst the second charts a new course.

The crux of the first interview is the heroine's confession that, for all her grief at Gaveston's death, her feelings for him had undergone a profound transformation:

> Je n'avais plus d'amour pour lui, mon frère; il avait trop su le bannir de mon cœur. Ses froideurs et le peu de confiance qu'il avait en moi m'ont cependant moins ulcérée que le fond de son caractère opiniâtre, avare et prodigue à la fois, vain, imprudent et emporté, ne m'a révoltée. Que j'en ai souffert! Je n'avais plus d'amour, non je n'en avais plus. Ah! mon frère, qu'il est affreux, qu'il est humiliant de ne plus estimer au fond de son cœur celui qu'on a choisi! (354–55)

This outburst is crucial to understanding the relationship between the Tencin and Beaumont texts. The heroine's *désamour* proceeds from the realisation that she could no longer 'esteem' Gaveston. *Amour* and *estime*: the association of these terms refers us to a literary tradition which proposes that real love is not an irrational passion but an appropriate response, emotional and rational, to the moral worth of the beloved.[17] In such a perspective, the heroine's past feelings for Gaveston cannot have been love, but only aberration and infatuation, and her subsequent *désamour* becomes an awakening to truth, an 'enlightenment' — as the heroine states, she has been 'éclairée trop tard sur l'objet de ma tendresse' (356). This reassessment of the past contradicts the Tencin tale. Far from being blind to Gaveston's true character, her heroine is all too aware of his shortcomings, and if she falls for his suspect charm, it is not because she is unenlightened, but through incapacity to direct her feelings. Here, it is important to note how closely the delineation of love in the Tencin tale follows that in *La Princesse de Clèves*. The words of the Princess — 'les passions peuvent me conduire; mais elles ne sauraient m'aveugler'[18] — apply perfectly to Mlle de Glocester. Each heroine's tale might be described as a progressive discovery of her feelings and of their object, but also of the very limited extent to which this process leads to control of these feelings or to real self-knowledge.

The nature and the implications of the self-knowledge which the Beaumont heroine achieves become clearer in the conclusion of the first interview. Mme de Cornouaille (the heroine's married name) confesses to her brother that the aspect of her situation which particularly afflicts her is that, as Gaveston's widow, she is disgracing her family:

> Ce qui m'accable à présent, c'est l'horreur de mon sort. Issue du sang des Glocester, nièce d'Edouard, votre sœur, celle de madame d'Herefort, veuve de [...] Gaveston! (356–57)

She apparently measures the aberrant nature of her passion by the fact that she, a daughter of the highest nobility, could have become the wife of so unworthy a person as Gaveston. Unworthy by his character or by his origins? The text is not explicit on this point, although the reference to her social position suggests the latter. In a century whose literature is marked by its questioning of the traditional nobilitarian equation of birth and worth, Beaumont's text seems to return us to a very conservative view of social position and *mésalliance*. However, the issue is not developed, but used instead to extend the heroine's revision of her past in another direction, towards a more general inculpation of female passion: her infatuation becomes not simply the story of an individual's mistakes, but a terrible example of the dangers of female passion in general ('Combien les dangers de cette passion sont terribles, pour notre sexe surtout!' (357)).

The Second Interview: the offer of marriage rejected

The second interview builds on the inculpation of female passion elaborated in the first. In explaining her rejection of Pembrocke's offer of marriage, Mme de Cornouaille returns to the disastrous social consequences of being Gaveston's widow, and to the likelihood that these would be shared by Pembrocke if he married her.[19] Imagining them married, she conjures up the most unbearable possibility of all, that Pembrocke might be affected by memories of the past, and by the tensions these caused:

> Je ne puis répondre d'ailleurs que je pusse, avec vous-même, dans les instans qui devraient être les plus doux, ne pas songer que ces idées cruelles [i.e. of social opprobrium caused by marriage to Gaveston's widow] pourraient venir quelquefois vous troubler. L'amour ne dure pas toujours [...]. (367)

'L'amour ne dure pas toujours [...].' The line returns us to the Princess's last interview with Nemours. One of the principal reasons she gives for not agreeing to marry him is that she cannot be certain that he will always love her. For the Princess, however, Nemours's future *désamour* is explicable by reference to his personality, and, more generally, to male affectivity.[20] The Beaumont text diverts responsibility away from the man and back to the woman. Pembrocke's future *désamour* would result from the impossible burden Mme de Cornouaille places upon him. It is not what he is, but what she has done that undermines any prospect of marriage: she chose Gaveston, her love for Gaveston brought about social confusion, and it is only in her abstention from remarriage that harmony can be restored. Her refusal to marry Pembrocke is an act of expiation for past errors ('Je dois expier mes anciennes erreurs' (369)). By contrast, whilst the Princess states that she has a duty to her late husband's memory, that *bienséance* requires that she forego contact with Nemours, and that she is indirectly responsible for her husband's death, she never explicitly expresses any sense of guilt, nor that she must expiate *erreurs*.

Where the interview in *La Princesse de Clèves* is marked by tentativeness and ambiguity, the Beaumont text offers a much simpler mapping out of motive and decision. In particular, the *refus* which, in *La Princesse de Clèves*, is so problematic in its origins and sense, becomes simple and irreversible.[21] It is prompted by a sense of guilt which is amplified by reference to a social 'order' which Mme de Cornouaille believes her past actions have imperilled and her future behaviour must restore — a dimension of guilt which has no clear equivalent in the Princess's case. I referred earlier to the conservative manner in which Beaumont treats the issue of social disparity. This conservatism manifests itself, more broadly, in the basic movement of her completion, which re-writes the tale she has inherited as one in which the stability of society has been disrupted by female 'passion', and then proposes a resolution which will restore this stability through female abnegation. We should also note that the same fundamental plot — disorder brought about by aberrant passion, enlightenment coming with *désamour*, and leading to restoration of social order — constitutes the basic articulation of Beaumont's major work, the *Lettres du Marquis de Rozelle*. There is a significant difference: in this novel, it is male 'passion' which threatens disorder, without, however, incurring the same condemnation as does the heroine's in the completion. Beaumont's conservatism thus appears distinctly 'gender-biased'. Male aberration is allowed resolution in marriage, procreation and family happiness, but female aberration seemingly requires redemption through abnegation and renunciation.

Beyond the 'refus'

The logic of Beaumont's re-orientation of the *Anecdotes* suggests the following ending: the guilt-ridden and penitent heroine, having turned down Pembrocke and committed herself to expiation of her *erreurs*, withdraws from the world. She does so, but only partially. Comparison with *La Princesse de Clèves* is again instructive: where the Princess, however tentatively, moves steadily away from the world, Mme de Cornouaille's widowhood does not lead to complete withdrawal from the world, but instead resolves into a stable accommodation of the social and the private realm. Whilst she holds to her refusal to marry Pembrocke, and partially retreats from the world, she maintains regular contact with both (she spends most of the year in a convent, and allows Pembrocke to visit her regularly. Her summers are spent on her married sister's estate, in touch with a wider society). This modus vivendi extends into an old age free of woe and guilt, in which the heroine's relationship with Pembrocke becomes ever deeper and more enriching. The novel concludes with one of the most emphatic celebrations of old age to be found in the eighteenth-century French novel.[22]

From this outline of the completion, we might infer that the author, true to her reputation, had taken as her task to divert the Tencin tale into a morally uplifting conclusion. Her heroine, guilty of having threatened social stability through her aberrant 'passion', renounces the chance of married happiness with Pembrocke, thereby atones for her *erreurs*, and is finally rewarded by an old age of peaceful satisfaction and clear conscience. Such a reading rests upon assumptions about female affectivity which are not simply conservative, in eighteenth-century terms, but distinctly misogynistic. The insistence on female passion as dangerous, the emphasis on its disruptive social effects, and the redemption of the widow through renunciation and expiation evoke attitudes of suspicion towards the daughters of Eve which can be traced from the medieval church to the more reactionary critics of the novel in the eighteenth century.

The modern reader will have difficulty with this reading of the completion, not because it might offend modern sensibilities, but because it seems at odds with an ending which is so clearly the celebration of a widowhood successfully organized and fully lived, rather than one eked out from repentance to reward. The misogyny implicit in the conservative reading, with its stress on the punishment of female affectivity and reward of womanly renunciation will, for most readers, be overwhelmed by the triumphant, even triumphalist tone of the concluding paragraphs. These difficulties of interpretation may be resolved by accepting that the completion works on two levels of reading. On one level, the Beaumont completion can be read by reference to a set of very conservative moral assumptions, but only at the cost of insufficiency of interpretation (it doesn't square with the concluding paragraphs). This insufficiency can, on the other hand, be resolved by a different reading of the moment in the text which founds the conservative reading, the heroine's refusal to marry Pembrocke. The climactic interview seems to require that we interpret the *refus* as a sacrifice. This interpretation in turn rests upon a more basic one, which assumes that marriage to Pembrocke must constitute the heroine's summum bonum.

If the notion of sacrifice is jettisoned, the apparent inconsistencies in the completion are largely resolved. The heroine's widowhood need no longer be thought of as expiation. It makes better sense in terms of her working out her own destiny (as she was not able to do either before or during her marriage). The private *béguinage* which she organizes for herself is marked by the control which it allows her over her life. Privacy is assured by the convent, and contact with the wider world is made on the heroine's terms. Order is restored, but it is not part of a wider return to social harmony. On the contrary, it is an order created by the heroine, an ordering of her own world, which stands contrasted to the turbulent world of court and politics. Finally, it is an order which rests, tacitly, on the refusal of the heterosexual couple as the fulfilment of a woman's life.

'La plus heureuse des femmes'

If the heroine's refusal of Pembrocke's offer is not a sacrifice, this must be because marriage to Pembrocke is not a fulfilment — and to accept this conclusion is apparently to deny the evidence of the text: 'je ne verrais que bonheur et délices à me donner à vous; je suis bien sûre, et je sens que je serais la plus heureuse des femmes' (364).[23] The happiest of wives or the happiest of women? The latter would seem the more natural reading. However, the happiest of wives is not necessarily the happiest of women, and the heroine, in declining Pembrocke's offer might be seen as politely refusing an offer to become what she no longer wants to be, a wife, in order to be what she wants to be, a woman.

This argument might be thought to depend upon a sophistical exploitation of the ambiguity of the French word *femme*. I would justify it by reference to the wider context of women's writing in the eighteenth century, and in particular to the feminocentric novel of the latter part of the century, as elaborated by novelists such as Le Prince de Beaumont (no relative) and Riccoboni. What marks these novelists is their apparent moral conservatism. At the same time, however, the dominant voice of moral orthodoxy which is so often evident in their novels may allow another voice to come through.[24] So it is with Beaumont's completion. A novelist with a reputation for conservatism in matters social and moral completes the unfinished work of a notoriously non-conformist writer, and does so by dragging her predecessor's story to a conclusion determined by interpretative cues which invite a conservative and even misogynistic reading. At the same time, however, the completion allows an alternative reading which affirms female autonomy, and proposes a misogamous rather than misogynist reading. The valorisation of female celibacy and the ambiguity in which it is expressed need not surprise us. They constitute distinctive aspects of the feminocentric fiction of the second part of the French eighteenth century. The heroine's progression, even when it is articulated through the highly conservative ideological norms of a writer like Beaumont, is marked by two features: a search for fulfilment which rejects marriage as a satisfactory means to this end, and recourse to ambiguity and obliquity in formulating and achieving this fulfilment.

KING'S COLLEGE, LONDON

NOTES

1.   A good overview of recent work on French female novelists of the late-seventeenth and eighteenth century may be obtained from *French Women Writers: a Bio-Bibliographical Source Book*, ed. by Eva Martin Sartori and Dorothy Wynne Zimmermann (New York, Westport, CT & London: 1991). The entries on Aulnoy, Graffigny, Riccoboni and Villedieu show both the strength and direction of the renewal of critical interest. The importance of the women novelists of the second half of the eighteenth century has been forcefully demonstrated by Joan Hynde Stewart in *Gynographs: French Novels by Women of the Late Eighteenth Century* (Lincoln, NE, & London: 1993). On the revision of the novel canon, and on the implications of this revision, see 'Men's Reading, Women's Writing: Gender and the Rise of the Novel', *Yale French Studies*, 75 (1988), 40–55.

2.   Claudine-Alexandrine Guérin de Tencin (1682–1749) was compelled by her parents to become a nun, took her vows at the age of sixteen, and immediately launched into a sustained attempt to be released from them. She succeeded in doing so, and became one of the most influential women of her generation. She was the (unmarried)

mother of d'Alembert, and the driving force behind the political career of her brother, the ultramontanist cardinal, Pierre de Tencin.

3.   Tencin's two best remembered novels are the *Mémoires du Comte de Comminge* (1735) and *Le Siège de Calais, nouvelle historique* (The Hague: 1739).

4.   Anne-Louise Dumesnil, Dame Elie de Beaumont (1730–83), *Lettres du Marquis de Roselle par Mme**** (London & Paris: 1764). Joan Hynde Stewart devotes a chapter to this work in *Gynographs*.

5.   The *Mercure de France* of May 1786, reviewing the *Lettres du Marquis de Roselle par Mme**** (pp. 23–38), devotes the last five pages of the review to an encomium of Beaumont, stressing her domestic virtues, altruism and self-abnegation. On page 37, expressions such as 'immoler ses goûts', 'renonçoit à ses volontés', 's'offrir comme victime' are used to characterize her personality.

6.   References to the *Anecdotes* are taken from the *Œuvres complètes de Mesdames de La Fayette, de Tencin et de Fontaines*, ed. by Etienne and A. Jay, 5 vols (Paris: 1825). The *Anecdotes* appear in the fifth volume. The first two parts of the novel are by Tencin, the third and last by Beaumont.

7.   'Galant' historical fiction is defined by Maurice Lever, *Le Roman français au XVIf siècle* (Paris: 1981), p. 201. The development of the *nouvelle historique* in the eighteenth century has been charted by René Godenne, *Histoire de la nouvelle française aux XVIf et XVIIf siècles* (Geneva: 1970).

8.   She was Margaret de Clare, daughter of the Earl of Gloucester. She married Gaveston in 1307. He died in 1312. The novel is for the most part a third-person narrative, centred upon the heroine, with a lengthy first-person retrospective account of the origins of her relationship to Gaveston occupying most of the first part.

9.   The historical original was Aymer de Valence, Earl of Pembroke, one of Gaveston's bitterest opponents, who took Gaveston into custody after his capture by Edward's rebellious barons, but was not implicated in his murder.

10.   The significance of the Nemours-Clèves opposition, and its wider context are examined by Jules Brody, 'La Princesse de Clèves and the myth of courtly love', *University of Toronto Quarterly*, 38I (1969), 105–35.

11.   On the complexities of this issue in *La Princesse de Clèves*, see John Dunlop, 'The Cloud of Unknowing: Self-Discovery in "La Princesse de Clèves"', *French Studies*, 48 (1994), 402–15.

12.   The Tencin *Anecdotes* did not end with Mlle de Glocester's tale, but diverted into a sub-plot involving a different set of characters. Beaumont winds up this sub-plot, and returns to the principal story-line.

13.   The 'galant' historical novel was never hamstrung by scrupulous historical exacti-
      tude, but the invention or suppression of marriages was unusual. The broad rule held
      that motives and private meetings might be invented, but that recorded events (e.g.
      births, deaths and marriages) must be respected.

14.   As the daughter and heiress of one of the greatest families in the kingdom, she was
      too important politically to be allowed the luxury of choosing her future.

15.   The 'formula' may be illustrated by reference to Marguerite de Lussan's *Marie
      d'Angleterre, reine-duchesse* (1749), which takes Henry VIII's sister as its heroine. She
      was married to Louis XII, and, after his death, to Henry's favourite, Charles
      Brandon, Duke of Suffolk. The Lussan re-working of history makes the second
      marriage a love-match which compensates the heroine for her dutiful acquiescence in
      the first, politically inspired marriage.

16.   She promises a dying friend that she will marry Gaveston, and comes under heavy
      pressure from her family and from the King to do so.

17.   This conception of love found its fullest expression in prose-fiction with the heroic
      novel of the seventeenth century. See Mark Bannister, *Privileged Mortals, The French
      Heroic Novel 1630–1660* (Oxford: 1983).

18.   Mme de Lafayette, *Romans et Nouvelles*, ed. E. Magne (Paris: 1970), p. 387. The words
      are spoken during the final interview with Nemours.

19.   His family would be repelled, the public would see her as 'la femme la plus fausse'
      and him as 'l'homme le plus faible' (367).

20.   *La Princesse de Clèves*, p. 387: the heroine cites both the general principle ('Mais les
      hommes conservent-ils de la passion dans ces engagements éternels?') and the particu-
      lar reference to Nemours ('vous êtes né avec toutes les dispositions pour la galanterie
      et toutes les qualités qui sont propres à y donner des succès heureux').

21.   On the nature of the *refus*, see Henri Coulet, 'Sur le dénouement de *La Princesse de
      Clèves*', in *Littératures classiques. Mme de La Fayette*, La Princesse de Montpensier, La
      Princesse de Clèves, ed. by Roger Duchêne and Pierre Ronzeaud (Paris: 1989), pp.
      79–85.

22.

> Tel fut enfin pour eux le pouvoir de la raison, de la sagesse, de la vertu et de
> la constante amitié, que, malgré les infortunes affreuses et accablantes de Mme
> de Cornouaille, malgré la passion toujours malheureuse de M. de Pembrocke,
> l'un et l'autre, sans faiblesse comme sans remords, passèrent une vie douce
> dans les temps les plus orageux, et parvinrent au seul bonheur qu'on puisse
> espérer dans la dernière vieillesse, celui du témoignage d'une âme pure, de la
> considération de ses proches, et des douceurs d'un attachement inaltérable.
> (373)

23. The statement is made to Pembrocke by the heroine, shortly before she declines his offer of marriage.

24. As Joan Hynde Stewart, in the conclusion to *Gynographes*, argues, '[women novelists] often said more than they seemed to be saying about the conventions they both used and lived' (p. 206). The conclusions to her chapters on Le Prince de Beaumont (Chapter 2, p. 49) and on Riccoboni (Chapter 4, p. 95) are particularly relevant to Elie de Beaumont.

C. P. Courtney

Construction of identity in the correspondence of Belle de Zuylen

The central theme of Belle de Zuylen's correspondence is the quest for identity — her own quest and the similar quest of her two major correspondents, Constant d'Hermenches and James Boswell. This quest generates a fascinating series of letters which not only explore a number of important problems, aesthetic, psychological and epistemological, but dramatize the search for identity in a way which is of compelling human interest.

Belle de Zuylen belonged to a milieu, that of the Dutch aristocracy, where one's identity was not normally seen as a problem;[1] it was something which had been settled by tradition. Belle, on occasion, refers to this tradition with approval, noting that she is proud to be a member of the noble van Tuyll family, which had never produced 'un homme lâche' or 'une femme galante' (28 October 1764 to Constant d'Hermenches, I, 333).[2] The ideal is a set of values where men and women have each clearly defined roles: men are to exhibit generosity and courage, women are to be chaste and virtuous. However, while Belle is capable, at least in certain moods, of speaking with admiration of this tradition, she is unable to resist pursuing lines of thought which in fact undermine it and bring into question particularly the identification of women, or at least the identification of Belle de Zuylen, with the accepted stereotype.

From an early age Belle was endowed with a remarkable intellectual curiosity and, although her formal education ended at the age of twelve, she continued to pursue her studies on her own initiative. She read French, English and Italian literature, studied history, theology and philosophy and took private lessons in mathematics and the natural sciences. Her aim, she tells us, is to acquire certainty in knowledge, and by certainty she means the kind of certainty one finds in mathematics, that is to say, 'des vérités évidentes et indisputables'. Comparing herself to Voltaire's Zadig, she says, 'L'arrangement que Dieu a mis dans l'univers est trop beau pour que je veuille l'ignorer' and she adds, with some feeling, 'Je n'aime pas les demi-connaissances' (25 February to 5 March 1764, to Constant d'Hermenches, I, 170).

In statements like this we have an important key to understanding Belle de Zuylen: hers is an eighteenth-century mind believing that philosophical and scientific enquiry will reveal a well-ordered universe where 'nature' and 'reason' are synonymous and where we have access to this cosmic order, not only through reason, but also (she tells us in many of her letters) through our natural feelings.

Since Belle's standards of judgement are based on 'reason' and 'nature', and since she is impatient with anything that falls short of absolute certainty, it follows that she is unable to identify herself with what she finds in a society where everything is based less on clearly demonstrated rational principles than on tradition, convention or on what she refers to with contempt as 'l'opinion', which in her vocabulary is more or less synonymous with blind prejudice, superstition or plain stupidity. And, since she was not afraid of expressing her views in public, it is not surprising she was not exactly popular, at least not with the more strait-laced members of her milieu, who considered her ill-mannered, if not something worse. It was known that on one occasion, at a ball given by the Prince of Orange, she had put herself forward in a most unladylike fashion and invited an army officer to dance, the officer in question being Colonel Constant d'Hermenches, a married man who lived more or less separated from his wife and whose reputation was that of a Don Juan. It was rumoured (and the rumour was accurate) that she even kept up a secret correspondence with d'Hermenches and a number of other men. It was widely known that she had published anonymously a *conte*[3] in the style of Voltaire in which she had satirized the nobility and that the book had been withdrawn from circulation by her outraged parents.

Needless to say, this kind of behaviour was not exactly designed to attract young men with conventional views who were looking for an obedient and submissive wife. James Boswell, who found Belle attractive, was intimidated; thus he writes in April 1764: 'She is a charming creature. But she is a *savante* and a *bel esprit*, and has published some things. She is much my superior. One does not like that' (Letter to William Johnson Temple, 17 April 1764, *Boswell in Holland*, p. 222).[4] And, a few days later, Boswell, having allowed himself to be convinced that Belle was not as intelligent as she appeared and that she was lacking in good sense, wrote: 'I thought it was a good thing. For if it were not for that lack, Zélide would have an absolute power. She would have unlimited dominion over men, and would overthrow the dignity of the male sex' (*Boswell in Holland*, 20 April 1764, pp. 224–25).

In the meantime, Belle was continuing to pursue her intellectual interests. But all was not well, for her hope that she might achieve certain knowledge was being constantly frustrated. Certainty might be available in mathematics, but her study of metaphysics and theology led only to uncertainty and doubt, the study of science bored her and seemed to lead nowhere and, as for moral philosophy, there was very little evidence, judging from the way men and women behaved, to show that they had any awareness of those principles which were supposed to be available to them either through reason or feeling.

But there was one area where, surely, it should be possible to find certainty: this was within oneself, one's own personality, knowledge of which should be available by introspection. Belle's *Portrait de Zélide*,[5] written in 1764 and circulated among her friends, is one such attempt at self-knowledge. However, it was not entirely successful; in the first place, she found that a pen-portrait, which by its nature is static, was inappropriate to something which was essentially mobile, that is to say to the constantly changing expression in her eyes and on her face and to similar changes in her thoughts and mood. She composed an addition to the portrait and then a second addition, but confessed that, however many self-portraits she might compose, no two would be exactly the same, and if none would be exactly true, none would be totally false.[6] Secondly, the attempt was not entirely successful because, since the work was to be read by a large number of people, it was not possible for Belle to express herself in a way which was totally uninhibited and which would reveal her deeper and more intimate feelings.

A more satisfactory solution was for her to express herself in private letters to someone she could trust. The letter form was flexible and well adapted to expressing changing moods; besides, since letters were private, she could say things she would prefer not to say in public. The correspondents she chose for this exercise were Constant d'Hermenches and James Boswell.

Her most important theme in these letters, the one which involved the greatest challenge to the conventional way of thinking, was her place as a young woman in society. Convention required that she should get married, have children and live happily ever after; this was the pattern accepted by Belle's female relatives and friends, many of whom, by the time she began writing to Boswell and d'Hermenches in the early 1760s, had settled down to a life of domesticity. Belle, true to her belief that in everything one should take *la raison* and *la nature* as guides, enquires into the status of marriage and comes to the conclusion that, at least as it exists in the society she knows, marriage is one of those artificial arrangements which is based, not on nature or reason, but on mere convention. It is a convention which, with its ideals of chastity and fidelity, takes little account of something which is given to a young woman by nature and which it is sheer hypocrisy to hide: her sexuality. This was, of course, a taboo subject, which respectable young women were not supposed to mention. Belle did mention it, in a letter to Boswell, who was profoundly shocked.[7] She tried again in letters to Constant d'Hermenches, and this time she was more fortunate: he encouraged her to speak out and she did so in a way which, by the standards of the period, is remarkable for its frankness.

What is most striking about these letters is, apart from their frankness, that Belle finds herself caught up in a typical eighteenth-century dilemma: the ambiguity of the terms 'nature' and 'natural'. If these are normative terms, synonymous with 'reason' and 'rational', it might be argued (at least by certain eighteenth-century theologians) that the convention of marriage is a perfectly natural arrangement reflecting at the human and social level something of the divine order which is to be found everywhere in the creation; without the institution of marriage, relations between the sexes would degenerate into disorder, with the consequence that society, based on the existence of the family, would be reduced to chaos. However, if 'nature' is taken in a non-normative or merely descriptive sense, then to follow nature is, quite logically, to espouse a philosophy of naturalism devoid of any moral imperatives. Belle wants to follow nature, including the promptings of her physical nature, and accepts that this means giving full rein to her sexual desires; 'Si je n'avais ni père ni mère je serais Ninon peut-être' she writes, indicating that, in her opinion the morals of Ninon de Lenclos, one of those *femmes galantes*' who had no representatives among her virtuous van Tuyll female ancestors, were in conformity with nature. However, could Belle really put these ideas into practice? Boswell, who was horrified when she used the term 'mistress', certainly thought not and wrote:

> Fie, Zélide! what fancies are these? Is a mistress half so agreeable a name as a wife? [...] I beseech you, never indulge such ideas. Respect mankind. Respect the institutions of society. If imagination presents gay caprice, be amused with it. But let reason reign. Conceal such ideas. Act with wisdom. (9 July 1764, I, 201)

Belle was reluctant to agree, though she admitted that, out of respect for her parents, she could not really take Ninon de Lenclos as a model. However, she found an ingenious solution to the dilemma, a solution hinted at in her letter to Boswell when she wrote, 'J'aimerais assez un mari qui me prendrait sur le pied de sa maîtresse'(14–17 June 1764, I, 191); in other words, she would indeed become a mistress, but her lover would quite simply be her husband. In this way all antinomies would be resolved; she would simultaneously satisfy her parents and discover her true identity; there would be perfect harmony between nature and convention, a kind of paradise on earth: 'Etre à la fois sage et voluptueuse,' she writes, 'répandre et trouver les fleurs du plaisir dans le lien du devoir, serait en effet la félicité céleste' (26 August 1764 to d'Hermenches, I, 278).

It is obvious, of course, that the kind of solution Belle had in mind depended on finding the right kind of husband. In fact, when she wrote the words quoted above, she had in mind a suitor who, she believed, would fit her requirements. This was the Marquis de Bellegarde, a man of ancient nobility and a high-ranking officer in the French army. She had only set eyes on Bellegarde once or twice, but he had been recommended to her by d'Hermenches who described the Marquis as his best friend and a man of exceptional personal qualities. It was true that Bellegarde was twenty years older than Belle, that he was a catholic, whereas her family was calvinist, and that he would require a large dowry in cash to pay his debts. However, since Bellegarde had been recommended by d'Hermenches, Belle was not intimidated by his age, and as for the problems posed by matters of religion or finance, she felt sure that these could be resolved.

It would be inappropriate in the present context to tell the remarkable story of the Bellegarde affair, which dragged on for years and ended only when the Marquis withdrew his suit. What is relevant is that, whereas Belle was confident she had now found an answer to the problem of her identity, an identity which she defines within the framework of the optimistic rationalism of the period, in fact she now begins to behave in a way which shows she is governed, not by cool reason, but by a disordered imagination. She and d'Hermenches conspire together to bring about her marriage with Bellegarde, even though it is painfully obvious that the latter has very little interest in Belle and, from every point of view, is an unsuitable candidate for her hand. Before long the letters exchanged between the two conspirators read like letters from sentimental prose fiction: the plot is melodramatic and Belle and d'Hermenches, who write to each other as if they are characters in a novel, simply lose contact with reality. On the rare occasions when Belle actually meets Bellegarde, she is taken aback and can hardly bring herself to say a word to him: Bellegarde in the flesh has little resemblance to the Bellegarde invented by her imagination. And in fact it is the same with d'Hermenches; when the latter was about to leave Holland for good he suggested that Belle should meet him at a secret rendez-vous in The Hague. She agreed, anticipating that this was an occasion when she was destined to fall into the arms of the man to whom she had divulged all her most intimate secrets. In fact, when they met, nothing happened; Belle froze and was tongue-tided, d'Hermenches kept his distance. She suddenly realized that the real d'Hermenches, whom she had only seen half a dozen times in her life, was not the d'Hermenches of the fantasy world she had created in her letters. However, she decided that if her relations with d'Hermenches existed only at the level of a fantasy-ridden epistolary exchange, not at the level of reality, then so much the worse for reality: 'Eh bien, écrivons' is her succinct comment (letter of 4 or 5 December 1764, I, 358): it is more important for Belle that life should imitate art than art imitate life.

At this time she was conducting a rather similar correspondence with Boswell. The latter, who had arrived in Utrecht in 1763 to study law, had decided that he would reconstruct his personality in order to discover his true identity: the James Boswell who had hitherto wasted his time in dissipation would become a reformed character so that the 'real' Boswell would emerge. Thus, he wrote to a friend on 20 January 1764:

> No longer ago than last winter I was the ardent votary of pleasure, a gay sceptic who never looked beyond the present hour, a hero and philosopher in dissipation and vice. Now I am all devoted to prudence and morality. I am full of the dignity of human nature [...]. (*Boswell in Holland*, pp. 118–19)

This decision to renounce dissipation and to pursue virtue was the result of Boswell's recent meeting with Samuel Johnson, whom he now took as a model. In his journal of this period he would write, from time to time, 'Be Johnson' and it was clear that his aim was to become, like Johnson, 'a Great Man'. In order to achieve this aim it was important that he should scrutinize his conduct regularly, in fact, on a daily basis, in a diary. 'As a lady adjusts her dress before a mirror', he writes, 'a man adjusts his character by looking at his journal'.[8]

The Boswell who converses with Belle de Zuylen at this time and who writes to her is the Boswell whose persona is not that of the 'hero and philosopher in dissipation and vice' mentioned in the letter quoted above, but the new Boswell, the 'real' Boswell, whose model is Johnson and who signs himself 'Mentor' even after his departure from Holland, when he abandons his virtuous way of life and decides that, after all, the emergence of the 'real' James Boswell requires a less austere attitude to the pleasures of the flesh.

The correspondence between Belle and Boswell is, like that between Belle and d'Hermenches, not so much an exchange of letters between two real people as between two characters in a novel and it is not insignificant that they should use pseudonyms: Belle is Zélide, Boswell is Mentor and each, to the surprise of the modern reader, takes the constructed persona of the other seriously: Belle really thinks that Boswell is a paragon of virtue and Boswell really thinks that Belle is a young woman about to take a lover. The truth is, of course, that Boswell is the real libertine whereas for Belle libertinage exists only in her imagination.

As we read Belle's correspondence of this period we realize that she, d'Hermenches and Boswell are victims of what is best described as a form of *bovarysme*, that is to say of a tendency to live in a fantasy world.[9] Each of them seeks his or her identity by constructing a persona which, while it satisfies their imagination, cuts them off from reality. When the real world has to be confronted the result, for victims of *bovarysme*, can be comic, as in the case of Don Quixote, or tragic, as in the case of the heroine of Flaubert's novel. In the case of Boswell it is probably best described as comic; thus, after leaving Holland, when he finds that his conduct is somewhat unusual, he writes in his journal:

> I was rather too singular. Why not? I am in reality an original character. Let me moderate and cultivate my originality. [...] Let me then be Boswell and render him as fine a fellow as possible. (20 July 1764, *Grand Tour*, p. 28)

> Be self. Be original. Be happy. You *was* so, certainly. Add to this learning and taste and devotion and *retenue*. Marry not, but think to have fine Saxon girls, etc. (21 July 1794, *Grand Tour*, p. 29)[10]

As for Belle, reality kept breaking in, for example on those occasions when she realized that the Bellegarde whom she occasionally met was not quite the same as the Bellegarde who existed in her imagination; but it was not until he decided to withdraw his suit that she really had to face up to the consequences of the collapse of her dream-world. Her reaction belongs neither to tragedy nor to comedy: she simply accepts that she was mistaken, that she had been misled by her imagination and she can now view the whole affair with a certain ironic detachment. With a sense of relief she rejects the *bovarysme* which had caused her so much unhappiness and, simultaneously giving up philosophical speculation, finds what is perhaps best described as a kind of ontological security by turning her attention to mundane matters, enjoying the simple pleasures of life, which include visits to friends and relations in various parts of Holland, walks in the country and conversation with people whom Constant d'Hermenches considered totally unintellectual and boring. Indeed, d'Hermenches was outraged at this change; Belle was now identifying herself with people of no distinction whereas he was enjoying the company of the cream of the French aristocracy; he was also implementing a kind of Boswellian reform which would allow his 'true' identity to emerge, an identity which had been stifled by his mistaken choice of an earlier career among the Dutch, a dull race who were incapable of appreciating him at his proper worth. Belle's reaction to d'Hermenches's pompous form of *bovarysme* is simply to laugh and to reaffirm that she is perfectly happy in enjoying the company of her uncomplicated friends.[11]

We must take leave of Boswell and d'Hermenches at this point. The former never really discovered his identity; his journals are the fascinating record of his quest. D'Hermenches seems to have suffered more and more from paranoia and eventually disappeared from Belle's life. As for Belle herself, after the *mariage manqué* with Bellegarde, she attempted simply to come to terms with ordinary life and, after her marriage in 1771 to Charles-Emmanuel de Charrière, she settled down at Colombier, near Neuchâtel, intending to have children and to devote herself to simple domesticity. She wrote nothing, or at least published nothing, for nearly fifteen years.

This is not the place to give a detailed account of the re-emergence of Belle de Zuylen, now Isabelle de Charrière, as a writer. However, a few points can be noted, particularly with regard to those writings where she continues to explore the theme of identity. One of the most striking features of her maturity is that, instead of turning her life into a novel, she has now achieved sufficient detachment to write proper novels, which can be read for their own sake without any biographical reference. But what is perhaps most significant is that she no longer examines the problem of identity simply within the framework of abstract ideas of nature and reason; instead, lowering her gaze, she examines it in the context of the society in which she lives; in the novels she published between 1784 and 1788 she writes, not from the lofty perspective of *la raison* and *la nature*, but from the perspective of how women are treated in eighteenth-century society, where the accepted values are loaded in favour of men. Indeed, she has now learned to distrust the kind of approach which starts off from first principles; in her youth, as we have seen, she wants to emulate Zadig, who, like Leibniz and Pope, believes in cosmic order; in her maturity she has become more like Candide, who has learned that blind faith in cosmic order is best left to people like Pangloss, while the rest of us will do better to get on with the ordinary business of living.

In many of the letters which in her later years she addresses to the numerous young people whom she had taken under her protection, Isabelle de Charrière warns them of the danger of losing their identity, or more precisely, of never achieving an identity. The danger lies in losing contact with reality, and this can come about in two ways: the first is by living in a fantasy or dream-world; the second is by being hyper-critical with regard to social conventions and rejecting offhand more or less everything that society has to offer. In these letters Isabelle de Charrière makes it quite clear that she is drawing on her own earlier experience; she now regards her *bovarysme* and her rejection of social conventions as the result of immaturity.[12]

She comes to the conclusion that individuals who cut themselves off from society, either through *bovarysme* or through a Panglossian addiction to higher philosophical principles, will never achieve a social or personal identity; they will remain isolated atoms and suffer from alienation. Human beings need each other and there can be no personal identity without shared values, values which are embedded in the traditions and conventions of the society in which they live. There is no point in rejecting these traditions and conventions because they do not conform to the higher principles of reason and nature, for Isabelle de Charrière, like Voltaire (the Voltaire of *Candide*) and like Hume, has come to realize that these higher principles are unknowable; the best we can do is 'cultiver notre jardin', a precept which she is fond of quoting and which sums up her final philosophy.[13] We can work to improve our lot, we can assume that even unphilosophical people know the difference between right and wrong, happiness and misery, but we have otherwise no direct access to any higher wisdom.

It would be interesting to pursue this analysis and particularly the affinity with thinkers like Voltaire and David Hume. Given that the epistemological framework is one where nothing is stable and all our values are constructs, one might ask, what is the status of the thing one refers to as one's identity? It, too, is surely nothing more than a construct. However, it is a construct without which life has no meaning. The search for identity is essentially a search for meaning in a world which we do not completely understand.

CHRIST'S COLLEGE, CAMBRIDGE

NOTES

1. See, for this milieu and for a general account of Belle de Zuylen, C. P. Courtney, *Isabelle de Charrière (Belle de Zuylen), a biography* (Oxford: The Voltaire Foundation, 1993).

2. References are to the following edition: Isabelle de Charrière/Belle de Zuylen, *Œuvres complètes*, 10 vols (Amsterdam: van Oorschot, 1979–84).

3. *Le Noble*, first published in 1763 (see *Œuvres complètes*, VIII, 13–14).

4. The reference is to *Boswell in Holland, 1763-1764, including his correspondence with Belle de Zuylen (Zélide)*, ed. by F. A. Pottle (New York: McGraw-Hill; London: Heinemann, 1952).

5. For the text of the *Portrait de Zélide*, see Courtney, *Biography*, pp. 738–40.

6.
> Vous le voulez donc, il faut revenir à Zélide. S'il ne s'agissait que de faire un autre tableau, la chose serait aisée. Ses amis disent qu'on en ferait vingt, tous ressemblants à l'original, tous différents entre eux.

Portrait de Zélide, in Courtney, *Biography*, p. 738.

7. Letter of 14-17 June 1764 (I, 189–92); it is to this letter that Boswell replies on 9 July 1764 (see extract quoted below).

8. Boswell's *Life of Johnson*, ed. by George Birkbeck Hill and L. F. Powell (Oxford: Clarendon Press, 1934), III, 228.

9.   See C. P. Courtney, 'Bovarysme et réalisme dans la correspondance de Belle de Zuylen', *CRIN* (*Cahiers de recherche des instituts néerlandais de langue et de littérature français ses*), 29 (1995), 15–22.

10.   The reference is to *Boswell on the Grand Tour: Germany and Switzerland, 1764*, ed. by F. A. Pottle (New York: McGraw-Hill; London: Heinemann, 1953).

11.   See, for this paragraph, Courtney, *Biography*, chapter XII, 'Resignation', pp. 229–40.

12.   See particularly her letters to Henriette L'Hardy and Isabelle de Gélieu, for example those discussed in Courtney, *Biography*, pp. 457–58, 464, 629.

13.   See for example, her letter of 13 May 1792 to Benjamin Constant:

> Comme Candide disait après toute sorte de raisonnements, 'il faut cultiver notre jardin', je vous aurais dit, il faut faire du bien quand nous pouvons, il faut tâcher de ne nuire à personne, il faut amuser notre esprit.

Benjamin Constant, *Correspondance générale*, vol. I, ed. C. P. Courtney and Dennis Wood (Tübingen: Niemeyer, 1993), p. 301.

The contributors

JUDITH BEALE studied Philosophy at University College and Bedford College London. She was called to the Bar in 1978 and continues to practice as a barrister, mostly in the fields of employment, sex discrimination and public law. In addition she studied French at Birkbeck College, where she obtained a BA in French in 1993 and is now working towards a PhD examining the changing representation of the self in French eighteenth-century prose fiction in the light of the theory of personal identity proposed by John Locke in the second edition (1694) of his *Essay concerning Human Understanding*.

ROSALIND BROWN-GRANT is Lecturer in French at Leeds University, specialising in medieval literature. She has written numerous articles on the early fifteenth-century author, Christine de Pizan, who is best known to modern readers for her texts in which she championed women against the tradition of literary misogyny which dominated medieval culture. Her monograph, *Reading Beyond Gender: Christine de Pizan and the Moral Defence of Women* is forthcoming with Cambridge University Press. She has just completed a new translation of Christine de Pizan's most famous anti-misogynist work, the *Book of the City of Ladies*, for Penguin Classics.

CECIL COURTNEY is Fellow of Christ's College, Cambridge, Emeritus Reader in French Intellectual History and Bibliography and Emeritus Leverhulme Fellow. His special interests are eighteenth-century thought, bibliography and publishing history. His publications include *A Bibliography of the Writings of Benjamin Constant* (London: MHRA, 1981) *Isabelle de Charrière (Belle de Zuylen), a Biography* (Oxford: Voltaire Foundation, 1989) and *Ma Vie* (Cambridge: Daemon Press, 1991). Co-editor of Isabelle de Charrière, *Oeuvres complètes* (Oxford: Voltaire Foundation, 1998 — in progress); General Editor of Benjamin Constant, *Correspondance générale* (Tübingen: Niemeyer, 1993 — in progress).

RENÉ DÉMORIS est professeur à l'Université de la Sorbonne Nouvelle — Paris III, où il est responsable du Centre de recherches sur l'esthétique des Lumières et de l'Ecole Doctorale. Il a publié plusieurs volumes et une soixantaine d'études portant sur la littérature du XVIIᵉ et du XVIIIᵉ siècles, en particulier sur le roman ainsi que sur la théorie de la peinture et la critique d'art.

En volume: *Le roman à la première personne du classicisme aux Lumières*, Paris. A. Colin, 1975. | Félibien: *Entretiens sur les vies et les ouvrages des plus excellents peintres*. Introduction, édition critique et notes. Belles Lettres, 1987. | *Lectures de ... Les fausses confidences de Marivaux. L'être et le paraître*. Paris Belin, 1987. | *Chardin, la chair et l'objet*. Adam Biro, 1991. | *Le silence de Manon*, coll. *Le texte rêve*, PUF, 1995.

Direction de publications: Saint-Réal: *De l'usage de l'histoire*. en coll. avec Christian Meurillon. GERL 17/18, 1980. | *La machine dans l'imaginaire (1650-1800)* en coll. avec Christian Meurillon. *Revue des sciences humaines*, 1982, n° 2-3. | *Les fins de la peinture*, (Actes du colloque du CERLAV 18.) Desjonquières, 1990. | *Hommage à Elizabeth Sophie Chéron, texte et peinture à l'âge classique*, PROSPECT n° 1. PSN, 1992. | *L'artiste en représentation dans la littérature française*, Desjonquières, 1993.

MARTIN HALL is Lecturer in French at King's College London. His principal interests lie in the eighteenth century, and he has published on Diderot and on the eighteenth-century French novel. A survey of eighteenth-century women novelists is due to be published in a collective volume on women writers, and current projects include a study of the influence of *La Princesse de Clèves* in the eighteenth century.

SHIRLEY JONES DAY was formerly Senior Lecturer in French at University College London where she is currently an Honorary Research Fellow. Her publications include numerous articles on the role of the woman novelist during the period from Mme de Lafayette to Mme de Tencin and a critical edition of Mme d'Aulnoy's *Histoire d'Hypolite, comte de Duglas* (1993). Her study of the generation of women novelists who were immediate successors of Madame de Lafayette, *The Search for Lyonnesse: Women's Fiction in France 1670–1703*, is due to appear shortly.

PATRICIA LOUETTE est ancienne allocataire de Paris III, Sorbonne nouvelle. Elle prépare une thèse sur Mme de Tencin (1682-1749). Elle a publié une étude sur 'Les voies/voix du désir dans *Les fous de Bassan* d'Anne Hébert (1982) — quel-

ques réflexions à propos du rapport à la mère: castration, dévoration et énonciation féminine'; et sur 'L'amour indigeste dans *Les Epices de la passion* d'Alfonso Arau adapté du roman de Laura Esquivel (*Para agua como chocolate*)'.

JONATHAN MALLINSON is Fellow and Tutor in French at Trinity College, Oxford. He has written extensively on the theatre and prose fiction of the seventeenth century, and his publications include *The comedies of Corneille* (1985), *Molière: 'L'Avare'* (1988) and a critical edition of Molière's *Misanthrope* (1996). He is currently writing a book on the seventeenth-century French novel.

MICHAEL MORIARTY is Professor of French Literature and Thought at Queen Mary and Westfield College, University of London. He was formerly a University Lecturer in French and Fellow of Gonville and Caius College, Cambridge. He has published *Taste and Ideology in Seventeenth-Century France* (Cambridge, 1988) and *Roland Barthes* (Cambridge, 1991), and various articles on seventeenth- and eighteenth-century French thought and literature, as well as on modern critical theory.